This visual notebook belongs to:

____

...But how am I supposed to use this book?

It's entirely up to you. A Visual Thinker's Notebook does not discriminate. Whether you're a writer, artist, innovator, brainstormer, deep thinker, doodler, or all of the above, the pages in this book, along with the accompanying prompts, will provoke your creativity to run wild.

For pages with lines (like the one to the right), it might feel natural to write in between them. But you might also feel like drawing or writing within the white triangular spaces, too — or instead. You can also flow your creations inside a tree or beneath the light shining inside a dark room. There are frames and signs and boxes and flames — all for you to interact with as you see fit.

Thirty distinct designs across 120 pages will give your mind the opportunity to take a completely different approach with every page you turn.

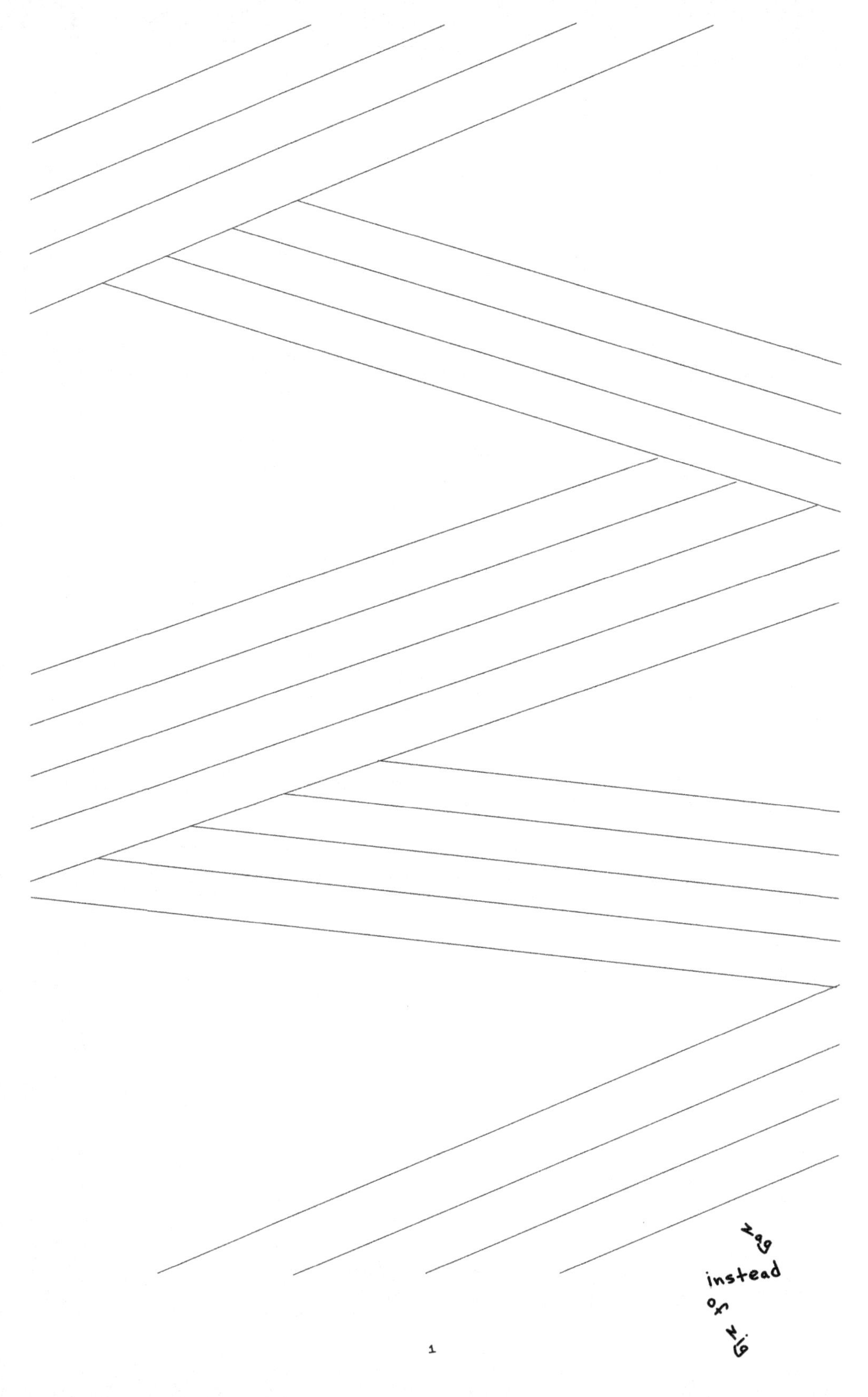

zag
instead
of
zig

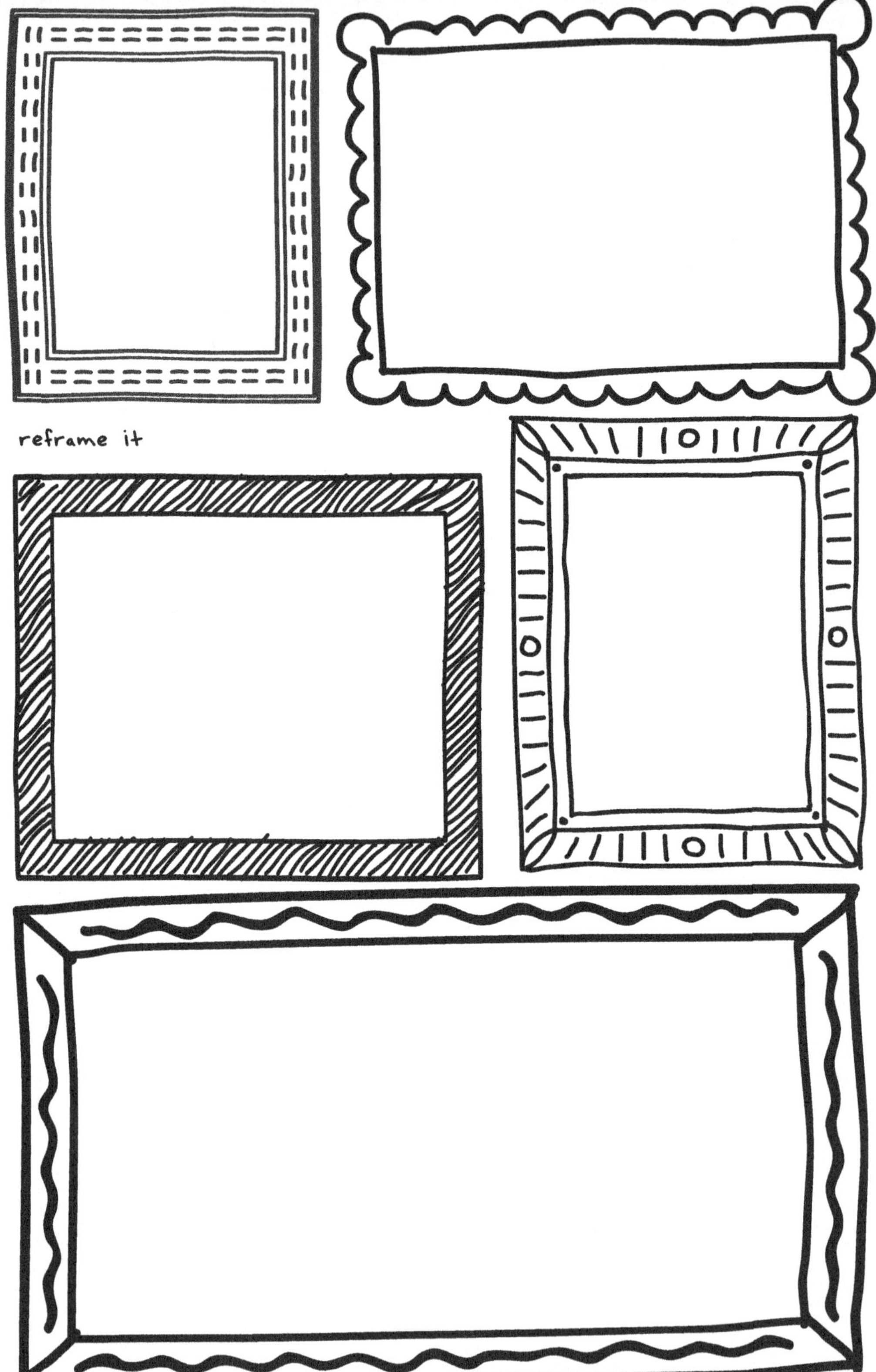
reframe it

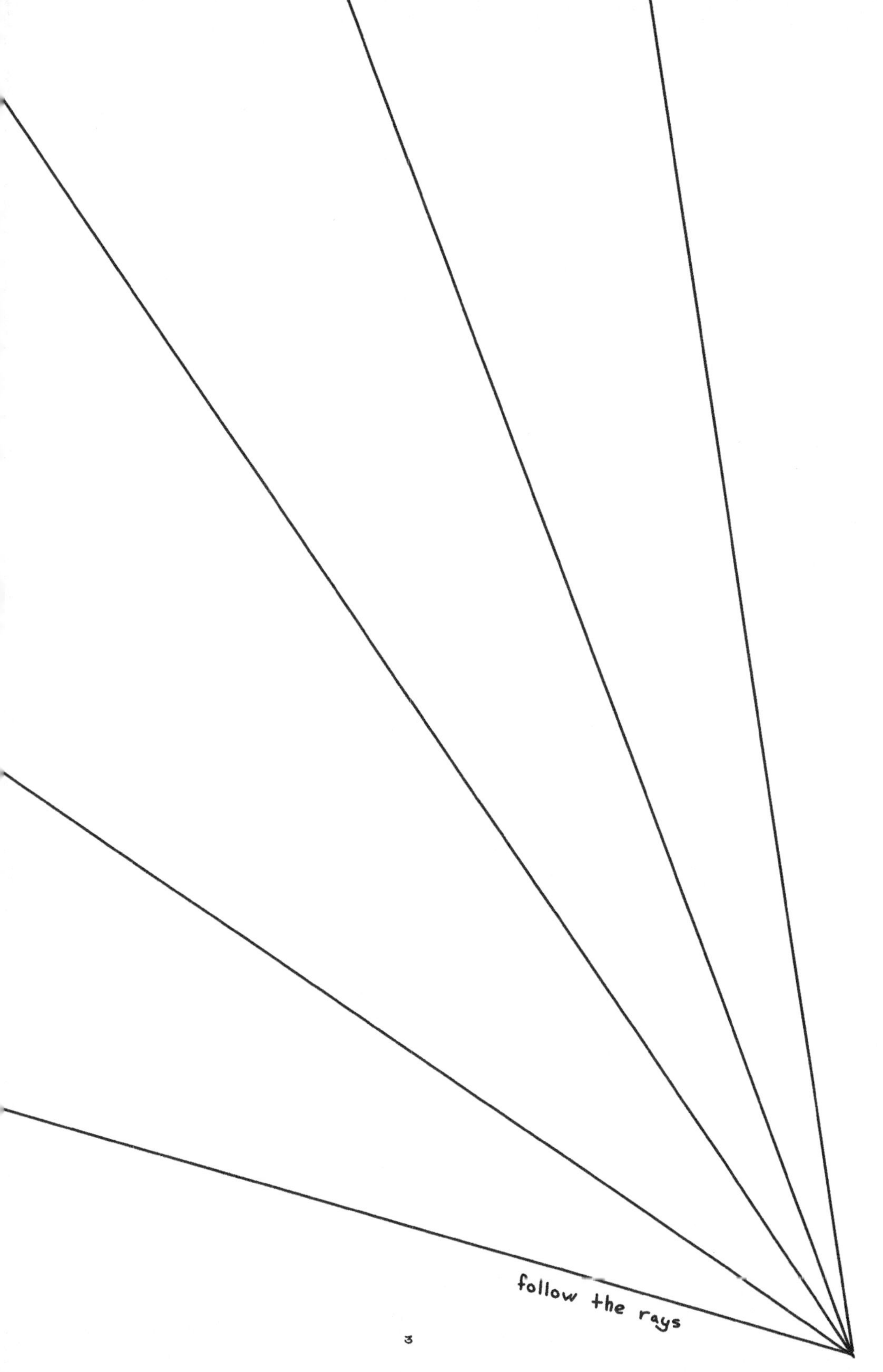

follow the rays

4

tilt
your
brain

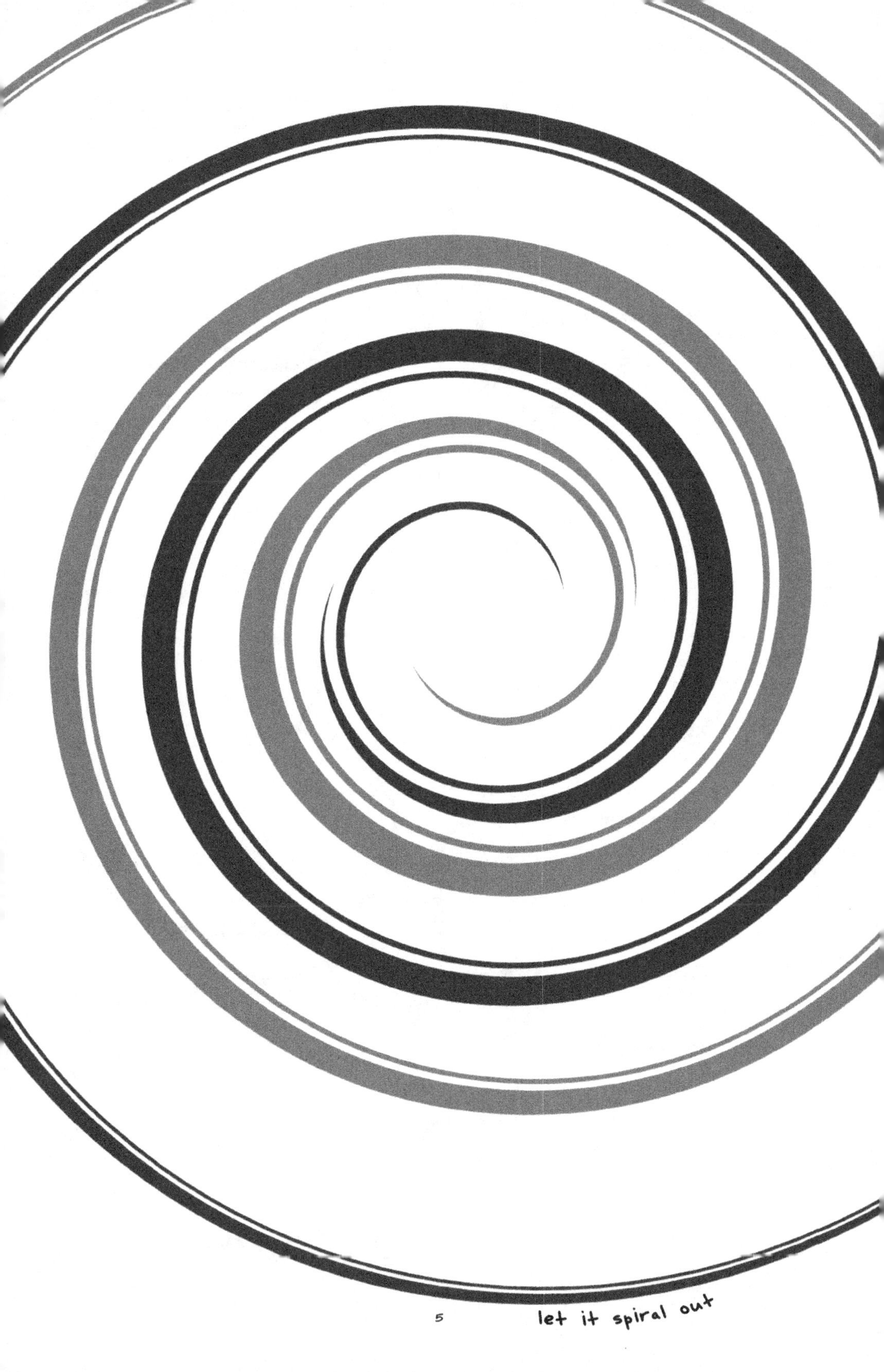
let it spiral out

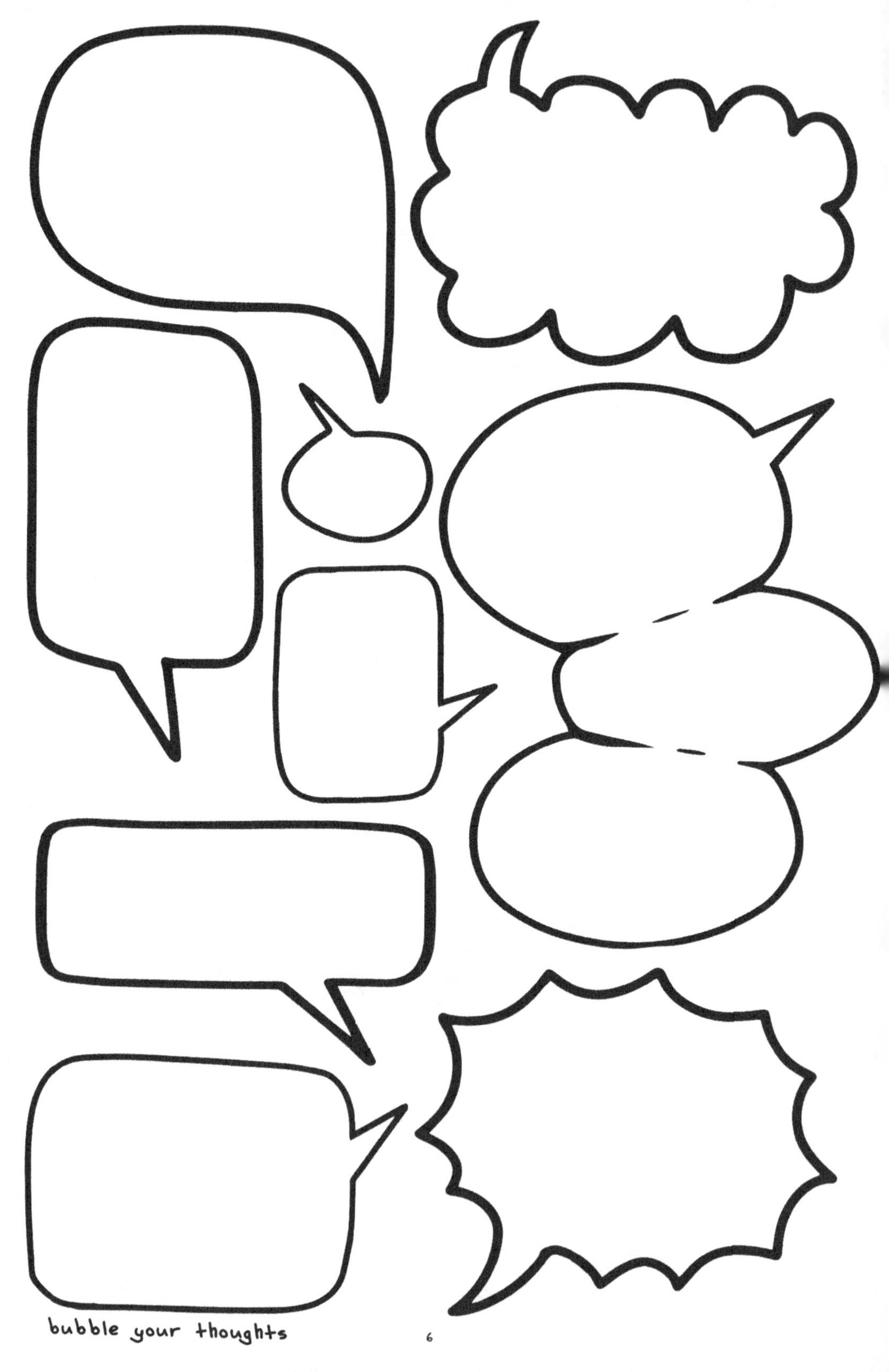
bubble your thoughts

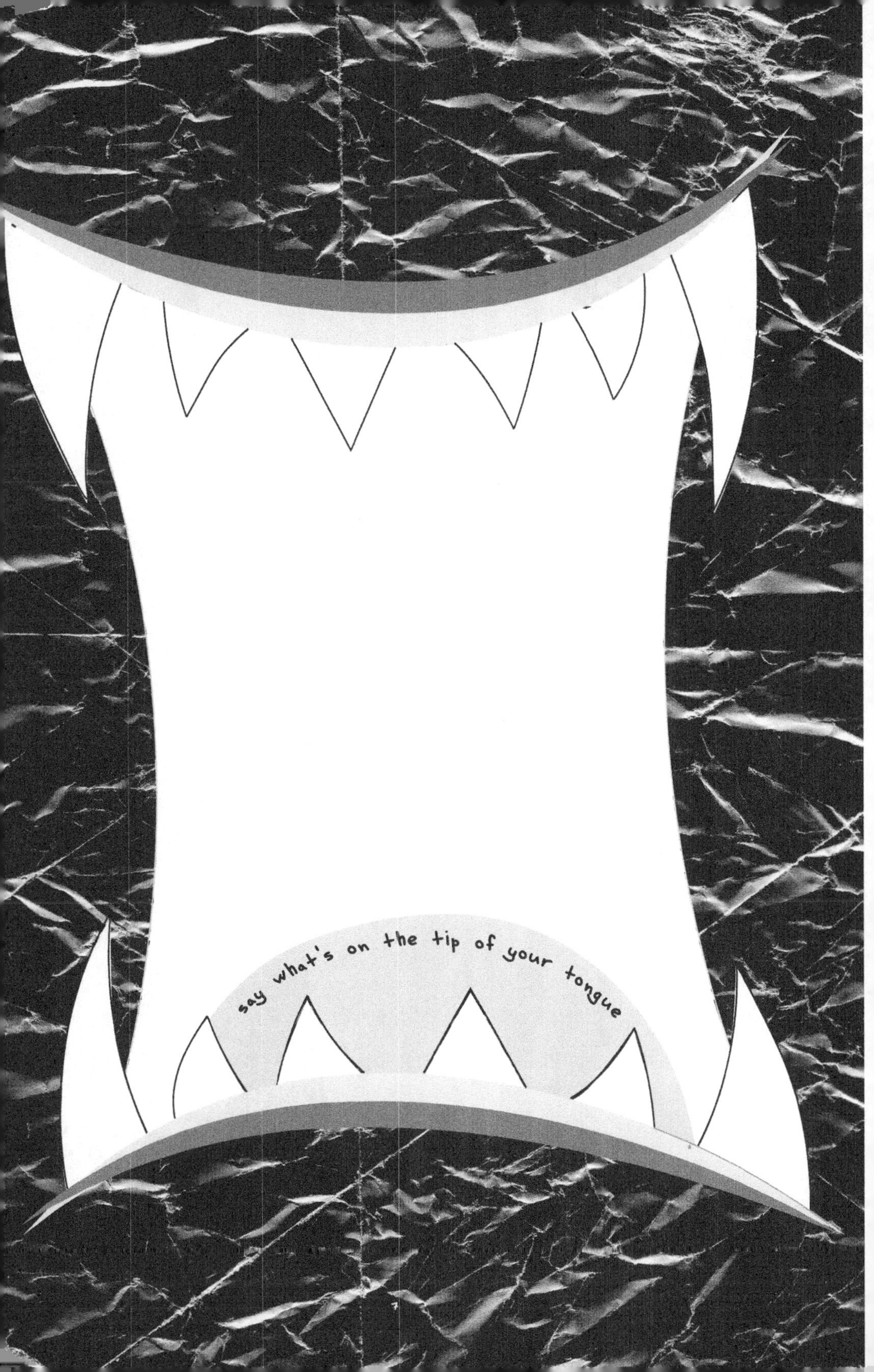

say what's on the tip of your tongue

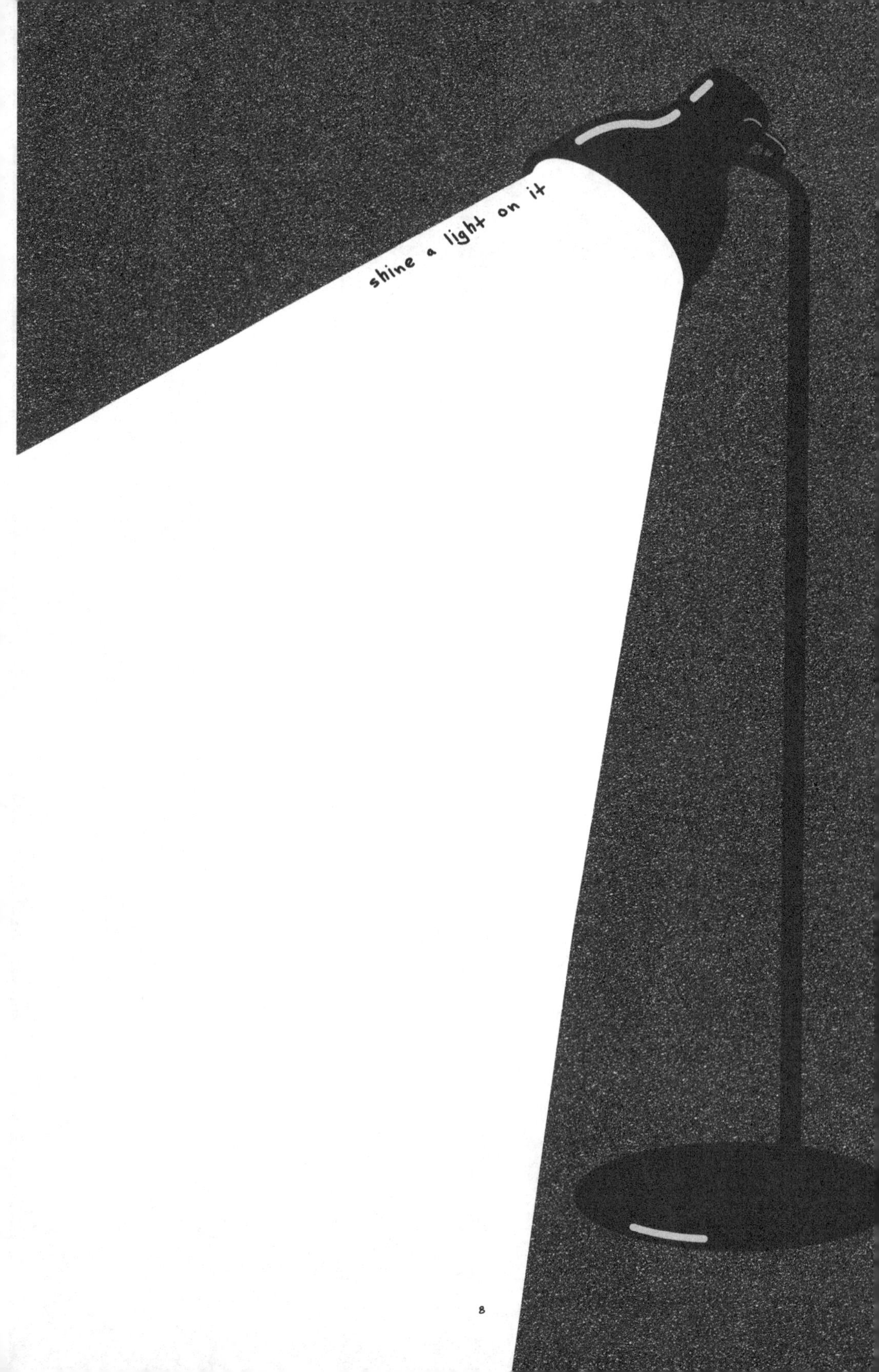
shine a light on it

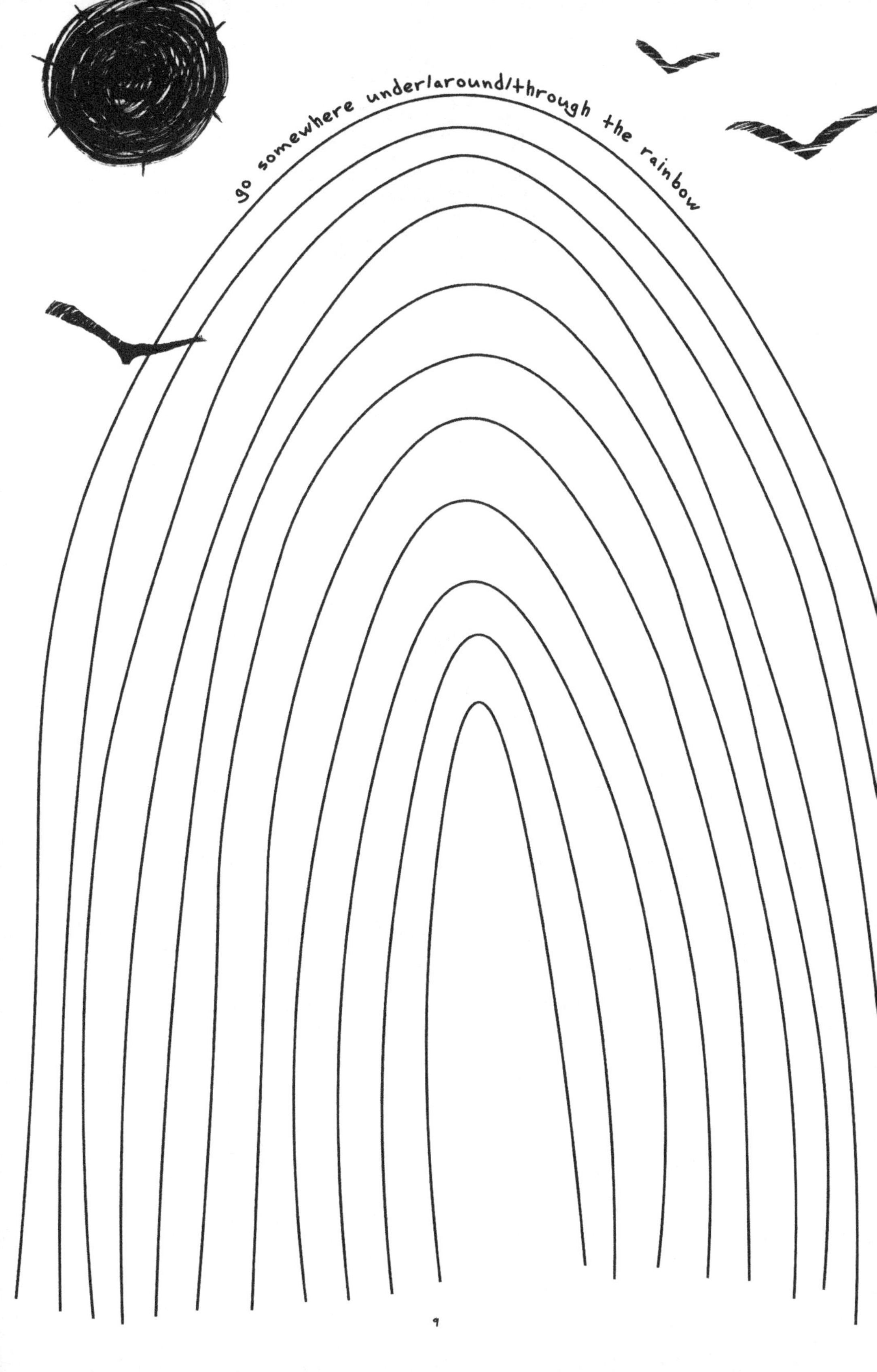
go somewhere under/around/through the rainbow

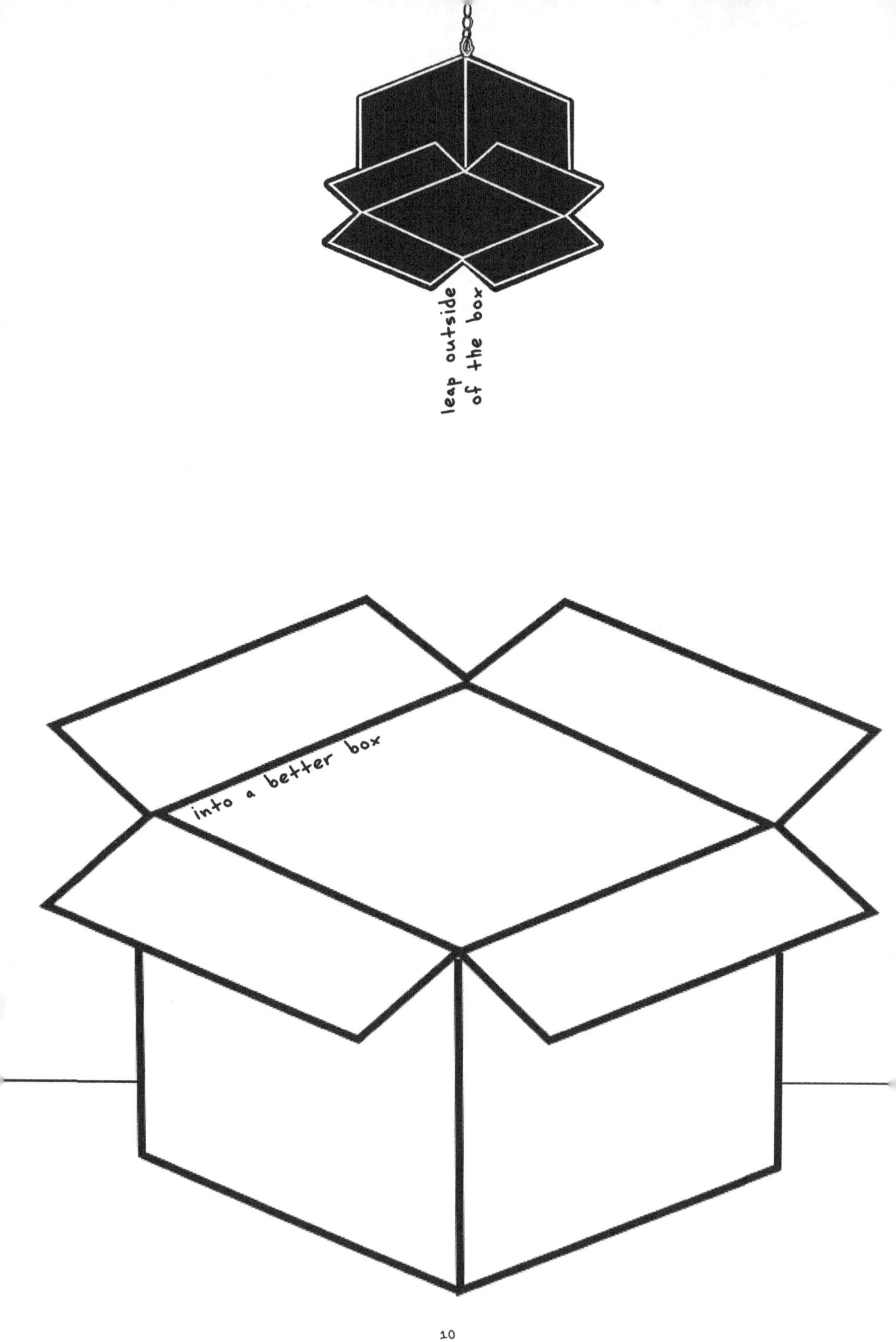

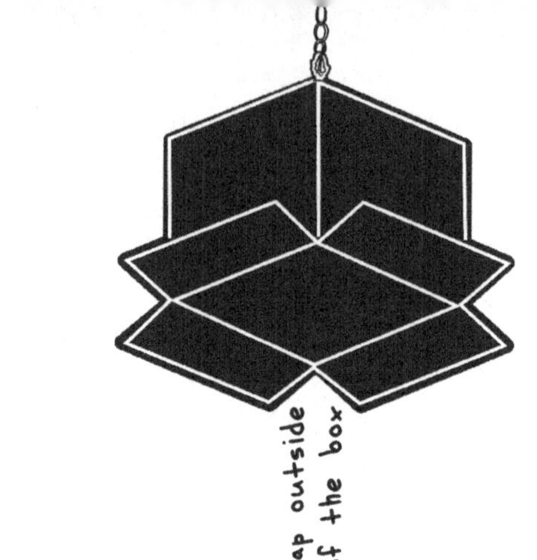

leap outside
of the box

into a better box

write yourself out of a corner

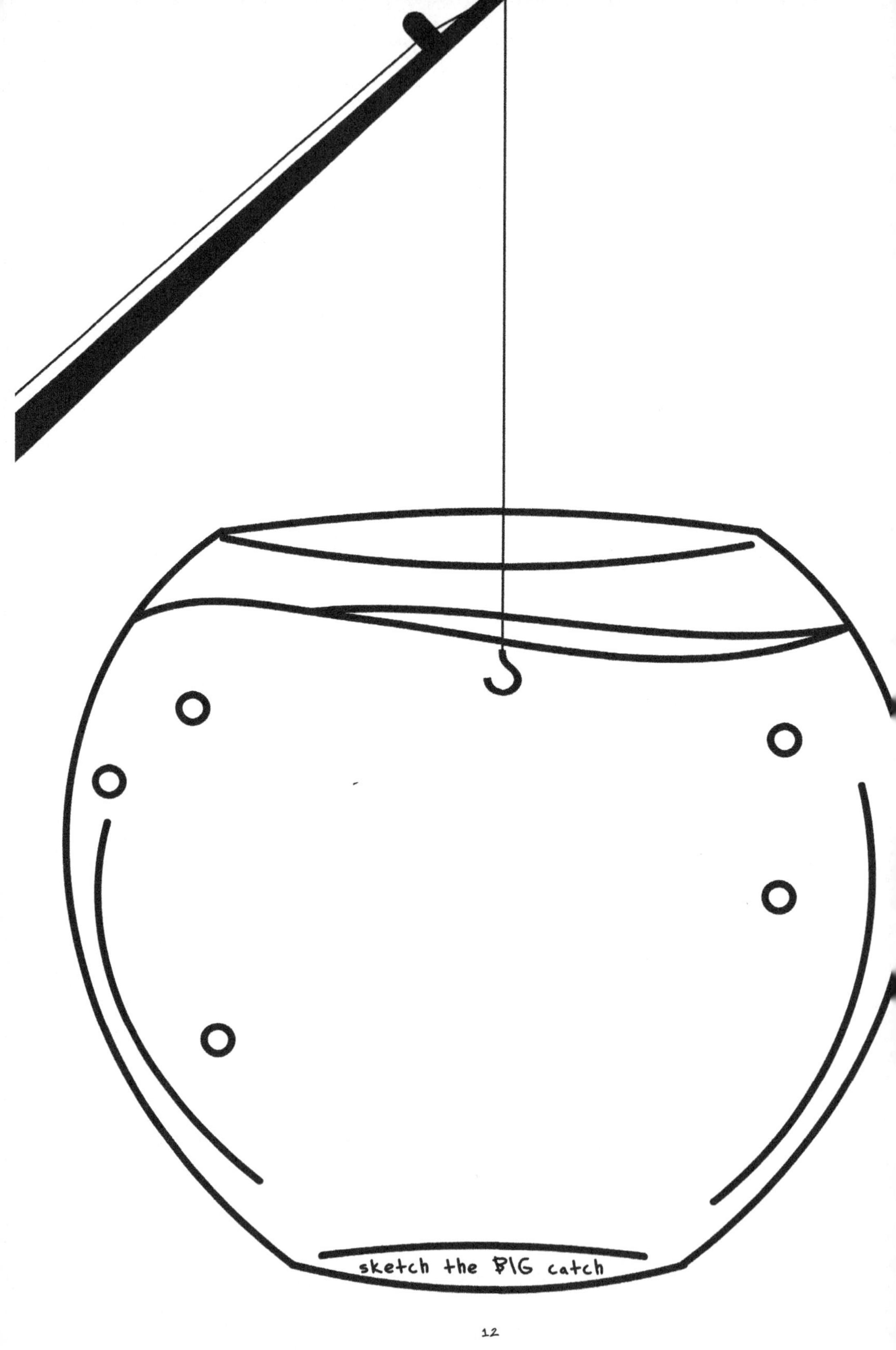

sketch the BIG catch

let it
take root

un-redact it

turn it upside down

negate the scribbles

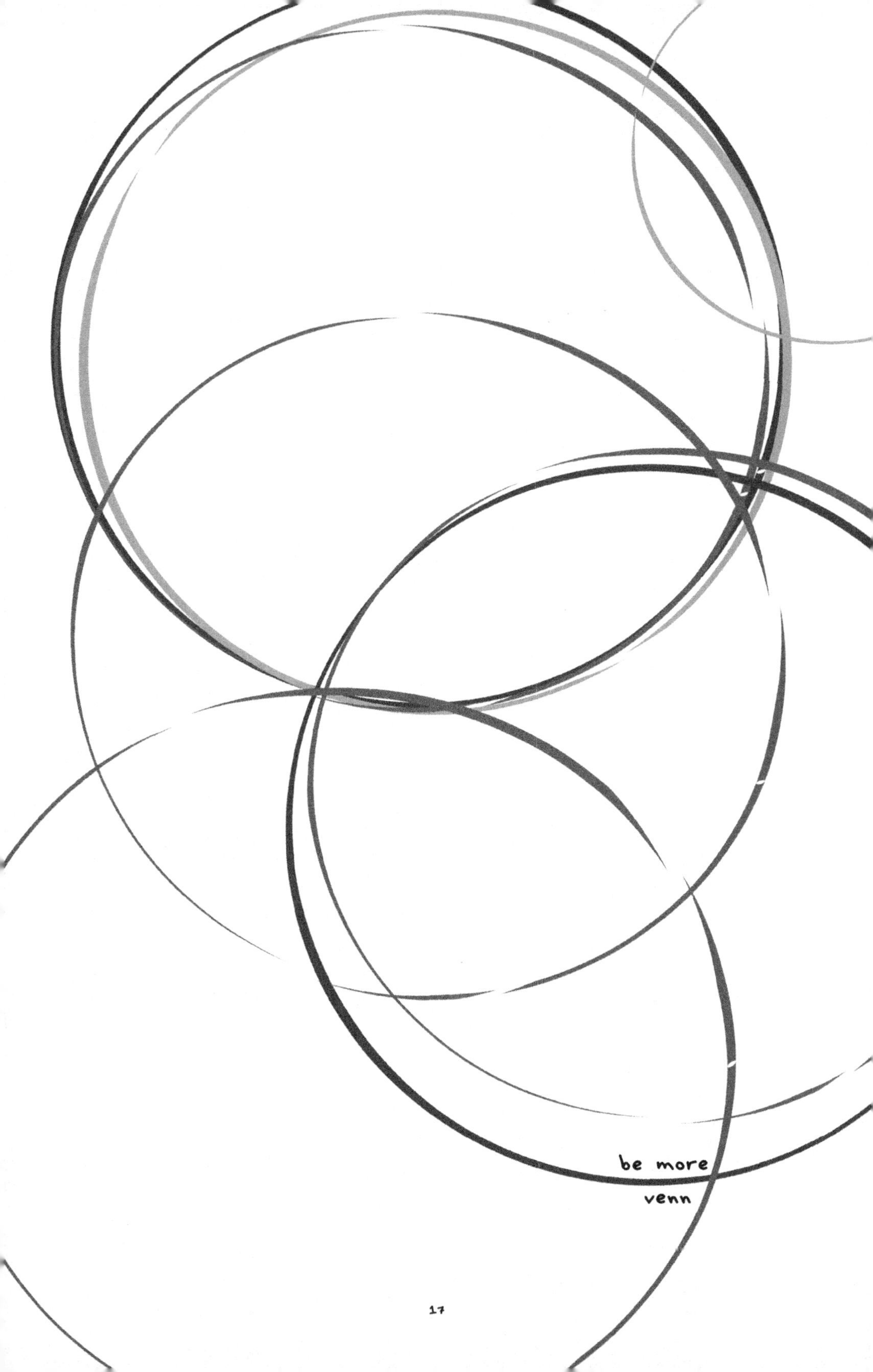

be more
venn

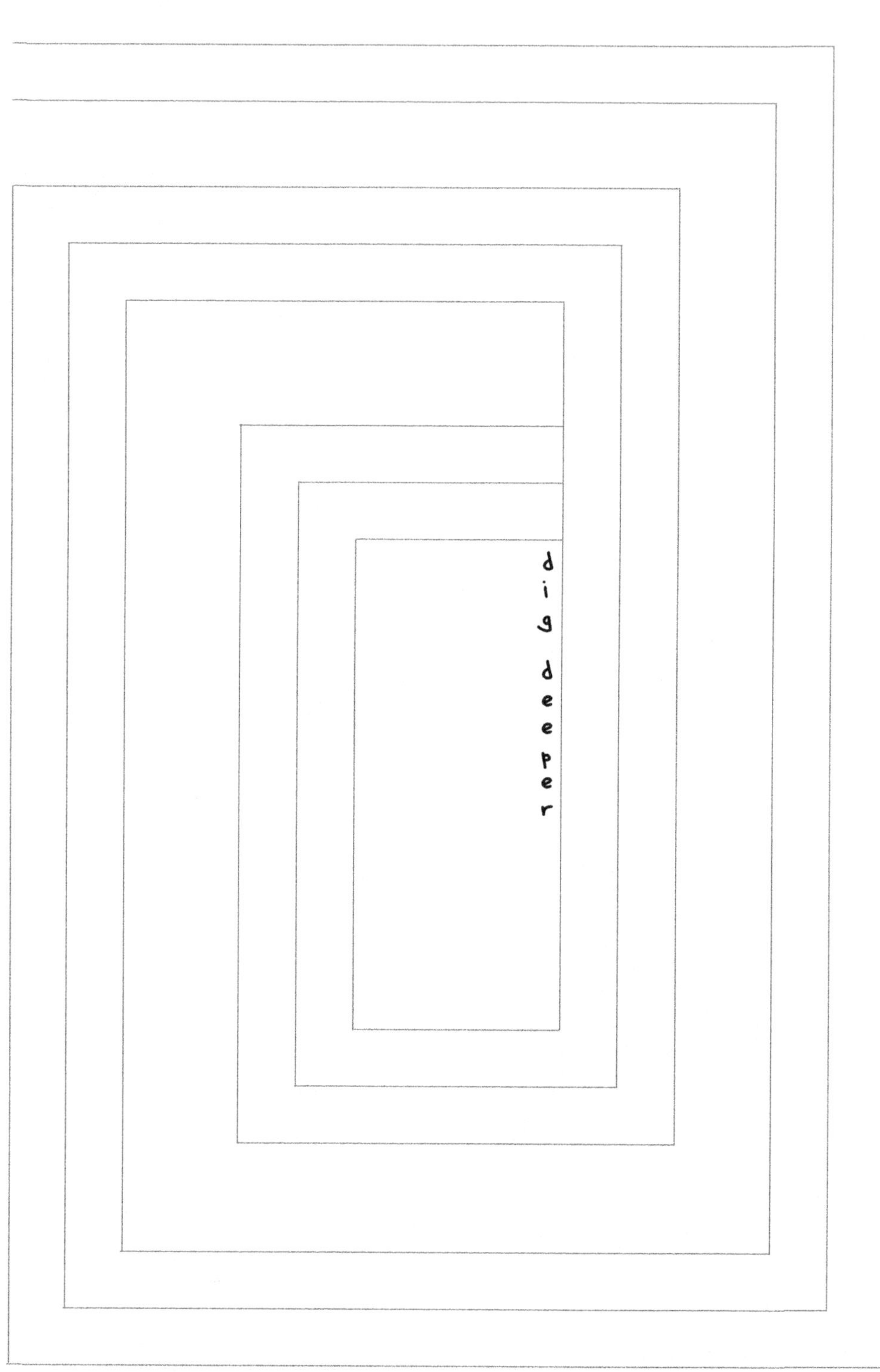
dig deeper

have a proper   brainstorm

vandalize it
vandalize it

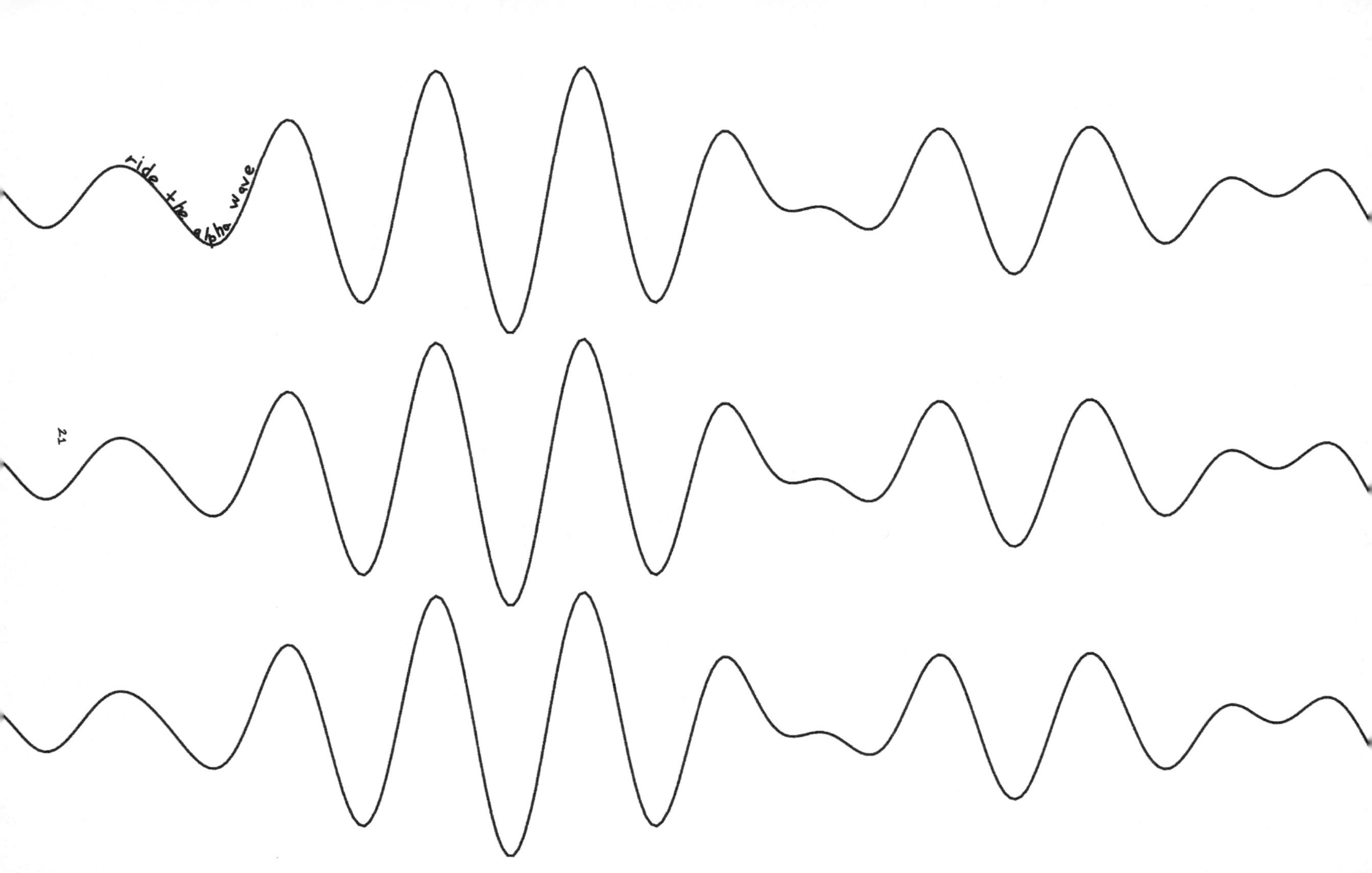

ride the alpha wave

set
it on
fire

AY.BLURT.SPILLIT.TELL.BEG.SCREAM.UTTER.PROCLAIM.EXPRESS.SPEAK.SHOUT.WHISPER.SPEW.AIRIT.YELL.CRYOUT.EXPLAIN.HOLLER.ECHO.BLARE.VOCALIZE.SPITITOUT.

TATE.PLEAD.BLABBER.MOUTH.COMMENT.SPOUT.REWORD.VENT.VOICE.DISCUSS.ARTICULATE.MUMBLE.SPIN.COMMENT.BLABBER.SAY.BLURT.REWORD.SPILLIT.ARTICULATE.TELL.

NNOUNCE.BEG.SNARL.SCREAM.ELABORATE.UTTER.PROCLAIM.VENT.EXPRESS.SPEAK.SPOUT.STATE.SHOUT.WHISPER.SPEW.PLEAD.AIR.YELL.CRYOUT.EXPLAIN.DECLARE.HOLLER.

ISCUSS.ECHO.BLARE.VOCALIZE.SPITITOUT.MOUTH.VOICE.ADMIT.SAY.BLURT.SPILLIT.TELL.BEG.SCREAM.UTTER.PROCLAIM.EXPRESS.SPEAK.SHOUT.WHISPER.SPEW.AIRIT.

ELL.CRYOUT.EXPLAIN.HOLLER.ECHO.BLARE.VOCALIZE.SPITITOUT.STATE.PLEAD.BLABBER.MOUTH.COMMENT.SPOUT.REWORD.VENT.VOICE.DISCUSS.ARTICULATE.MUMBLE.SPIN.

OMMENT.BLABBER.SAY.BLURT.REWORD.SPILLIT.ARTICULATE.TELL.ANNOUNCE.BEG.ADMIT.SNARL.SCREAM.ELABORATE.UTTER.PROCLAIM.VENT.EXPRESS.SPEAK.SPOUT.STATE.

HOUT.WHISPER.SPEW.PLEAD.AIR.YELL.CRYOUT.EXPLAIN.DECLARE.HOLLER.DISCUSS.ECHO.BLARE.VOCALIZE.SPITITOUT.MOUTH.VOICE.SAY.BLURT.SPILLIT.TELL.BEG.SCREAM.

TTER.PROCLAIM.EXPRESS.SPEAK.SHOUT.WHISPER.SPEW.AIRIT.YELL.CRYOUT.EXPLAIN.HOLLER.ECHO.BLARE.VOCALIZE.SPITITOUT.STATE.PLEAD.BLABBER.MOUTH.COMMENT.SPOUT.

EWORD.VENT.VOICE.DISCUSS.ARTICULATE.ADMIT.MUMBLE.SPIN.COMMENT.BLABBER.SAY.BLURT.REWORD.SPILLIT.ARTICULATE.TELL.ANNOUNCE.BEG.SNARL.SCREAM.ELABORATE.

TTER.PROCLAIM.VENT.EXPRESS.SPEAK.SPOUT.STATE.SHOUT.WHISPER.SPEW.PLEAD.AIR.YELL.CRYOUT.EXPLAIN.DECLARE.HOLLER.DISCUSS.ECHO.BLARE.VOCALIZE.SPITITOUT.

OUTH.VOICE.SAY.BLURT.SPILLIT.TELL.BEG.SCREAM.UTTER.PROCLAIM.EXPRESS.SPEAK.SHOUT.WHISPER.SPEW.AIRIT.YELL.CRYOUT.EXPLAIN.HOLLER.ECHO.BLARE.

OCALIZE.SPITITOUT.STATE.PLEAD.BLABBER.MOUTH.COMMENT.SPOUT.REWORD.VENT.VOICE.DISCUSS.ARTICULATE.MUMBLE.SPIN.COMMENT.BLABBER.SAY.BLURT.REWORD.SPILLIT.

RTICULATE.TELL.ANNOUNCE.BEG.SNARL.SCREAM.ELABORATE.UTTER.PROCLAIM.VENT.EXPRESS.SPEAK.SPOUT.STATE.SHOUT.WHISPER.SPEW.PLEAD.AIR.YELL.CRYOUT.

XPLAIN.DECLARE.HOLLER.DISCUSS.ECHO.BLARE.VOCALIZE.SPITITOUT.MOUTH.VOICE.SAY.BLURT.SPILLIT.SUGGEST.TELL.BEG.SCREAM.UTTER.PROCLAIM.EXPRESS.SPEAK.SHOUT.

HISPER.SPEW.AIRIT.YELL.CRYOUT.EXPLAIN.HOLLER.ECHO.BLARE.VOCALIZE.SPITITOUT.STATE.PLEAD.BLABBER.MOUTH.COMMENT.SPOUT.REWORD.VENT.VOICE.DISCUSS.

RTICULATE.MUMBLE.SPIN.COMMENT.BLABBER.SAY.BLURT.REWORD.SPILLIT.ARTICULATE.TELL.ANNOUNCE.BEG.SNARL.SCREAM.ELABORATE.UTTER.PROCLAIM.VENT.EXPRESS.SPEAK.

POUT.STATE.SHOUT.WHISPER.SPEW.PLEAD.AIR.YELL.CRYOUT.EXPLAIN.DECLARE.HOLLER.DISCUSS.ECHO.BLARE.VOCALIZE.SPITITOUT.MOUTH.VOICE.SAY.BLURT.SPILLIT.

ELL.BEG.SCREAM.UTTER.PROCLAIM.EXPRESS.SUGGEST.SPEAK.SHOUT.WHISPER.SPEW.AIRIT.YELL.CRYOUT.EXPLAIN.HOLLER.ECHO.BLARE.VOCALIZE.SPITITOUT.STATE.PLEAD.

BLABBER.ADMIT.MOUTH.COMMENT.SPOUT.REWORD.VENT.VOICE.DISCUSS.ARTICULATE.MUMBLE.SPIN.COMMENT.BLABBER.SAY.BLURT.REWORD.SPILLIT.ARTICULATE.TELL.

ANNOUNCE.BEG.SNARL.SCREAM.ELABORATE.UTTER.PROCLAIM.VENT.EXPRESS.SPEAK.SPOUT.STATE.SHOUT.WHISPER.SPEW.PLEAD.AIR.YELL.CRYOUT.EXPLAIN.SUGGEST.DECLARE.

HOLLER.DISCUSS.ECHO.BLARE.VOCALIZE.SPITITOUT.MOUTH.VOICE.SAY.BLURT.SPILLIT.TELL.BEG.SCREAM.UTTER.PROCLAIM.EXPRESS.SPEAK.SHOUT.WHISPER.SPEW.AIRIT.YELL.

CRYOUT.EXPLAIN.HOLLER.ECHO.ADMIT.BLARE.VOCALIZE.SPITITOUT.STATE.PLEAD.BLABBER.MOUTH.COMMENT.SPOUT.REWORD.VENT.VOICE.DISCUSS.ARTICULATE.MUMBLE.SPIN.

COMMENT.BLABBER.SAY.BLURT.REWORD.SPILLIT.ARTICULATE.TELL.ANNOUNCE.BEG.SNARL.SCREAM.ELABORATE.UTTER.PROCLAIM.VENT.EXPRESS.SPEAK.SPOUT.STATE.SHOUT.

WHISPER.ADMIT.SPEW.PLEAD.AIR.YELL.CRYOUT.EXPLAIN.DECLARE.HOLLER.DISCUSS.ECHO.BLARE.VOCALIZE.SPITITOUT.MOUTH.VOICE.SAY.BLURT.SPILLIT.TELL.BEG.SCREAM.

UTTER.PROCLAIM.EXPRESS.SPEAK.SHOUT.WHISPER.SPEW.AIRIT.YELL.CRYOUT.EXPLAIN.HOLLER.ECHO.BLARE.VOCALIZE.SPITITOUT.STATE.PLEAD.BLABBER.MOUTH.COMMENT.

think in between the lines

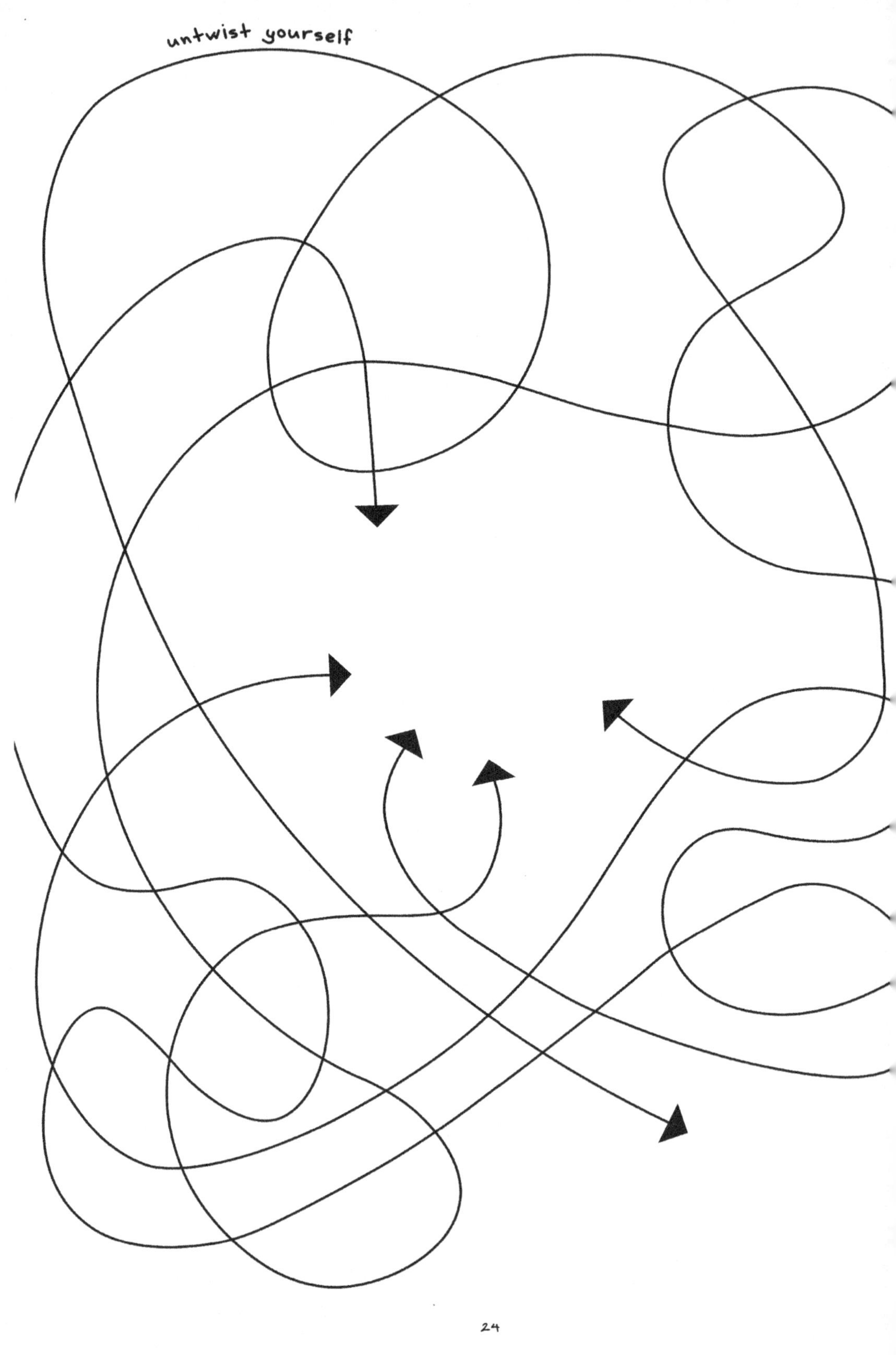
untwist yourself
untwist yourself

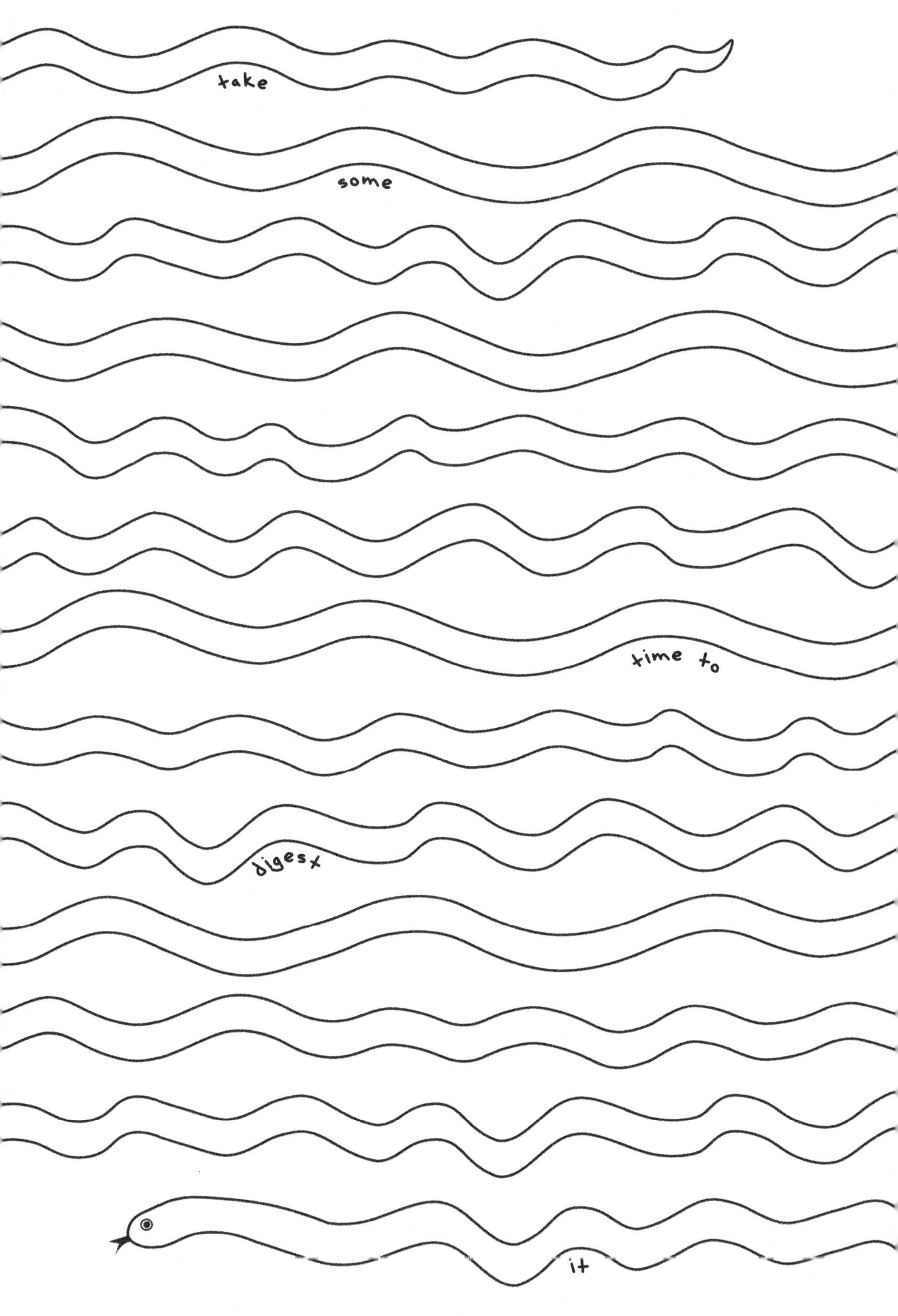

take
some
time to
digest
it

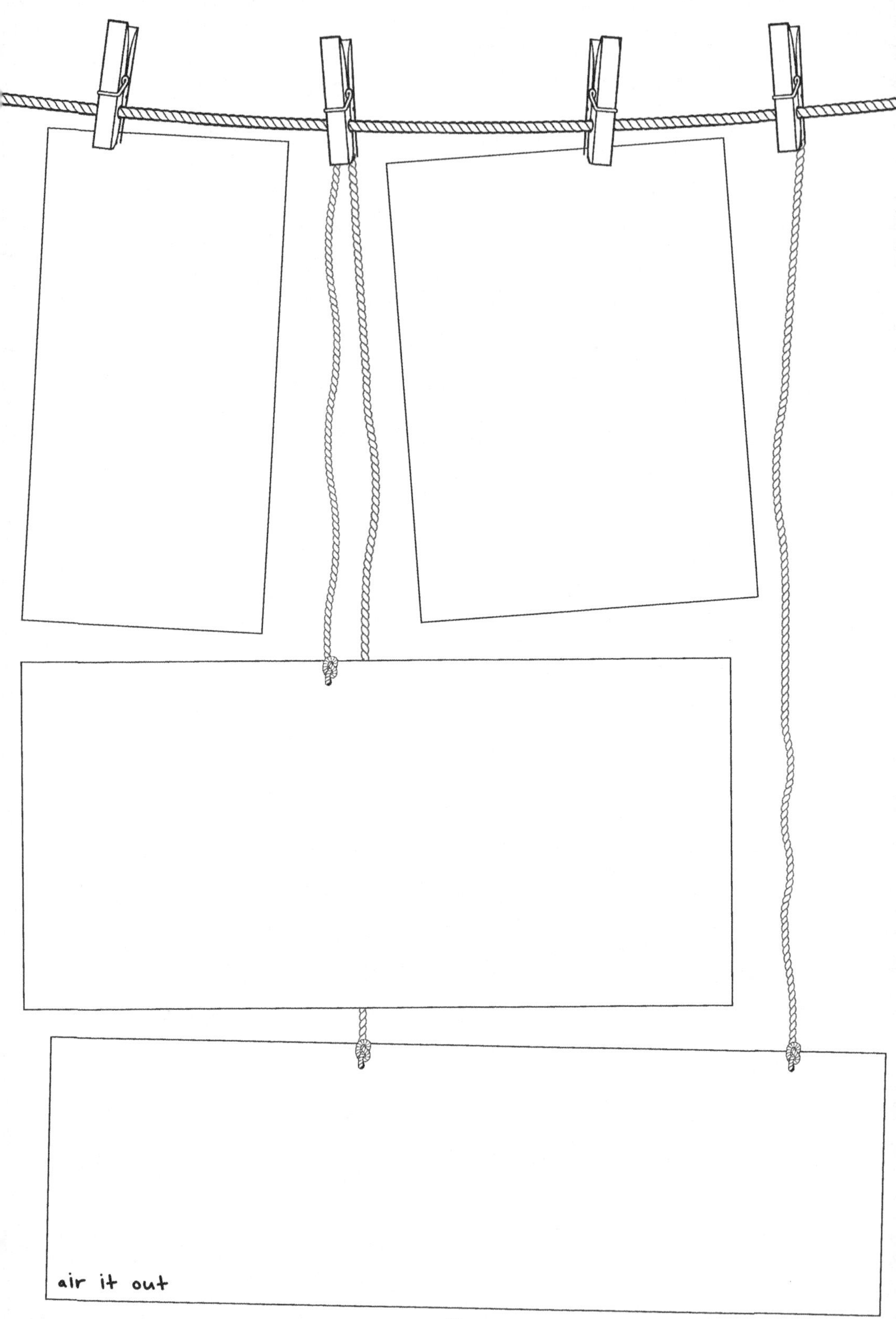
air it out
air it out

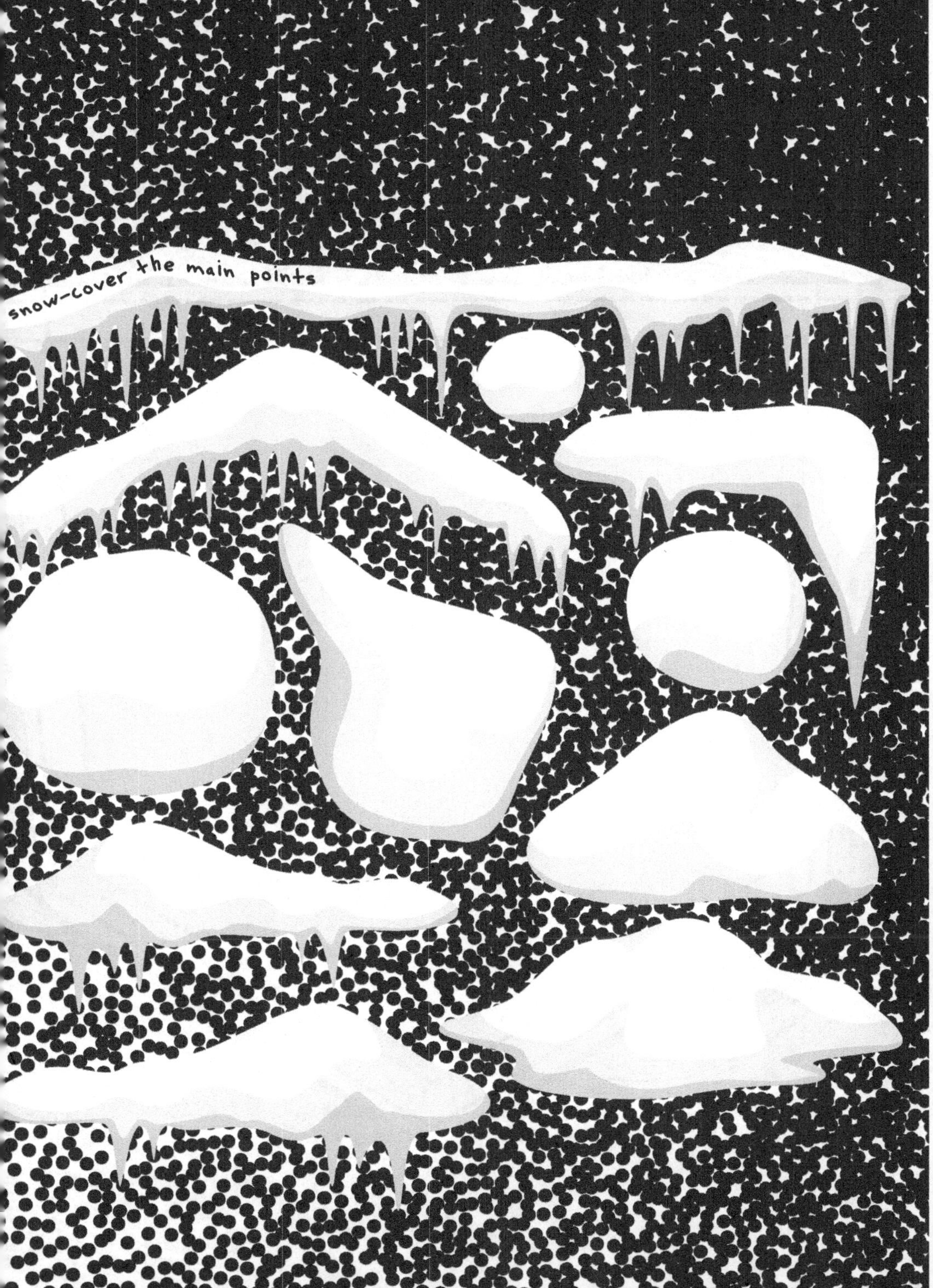

snow-cover the main points
snow-cover the main points

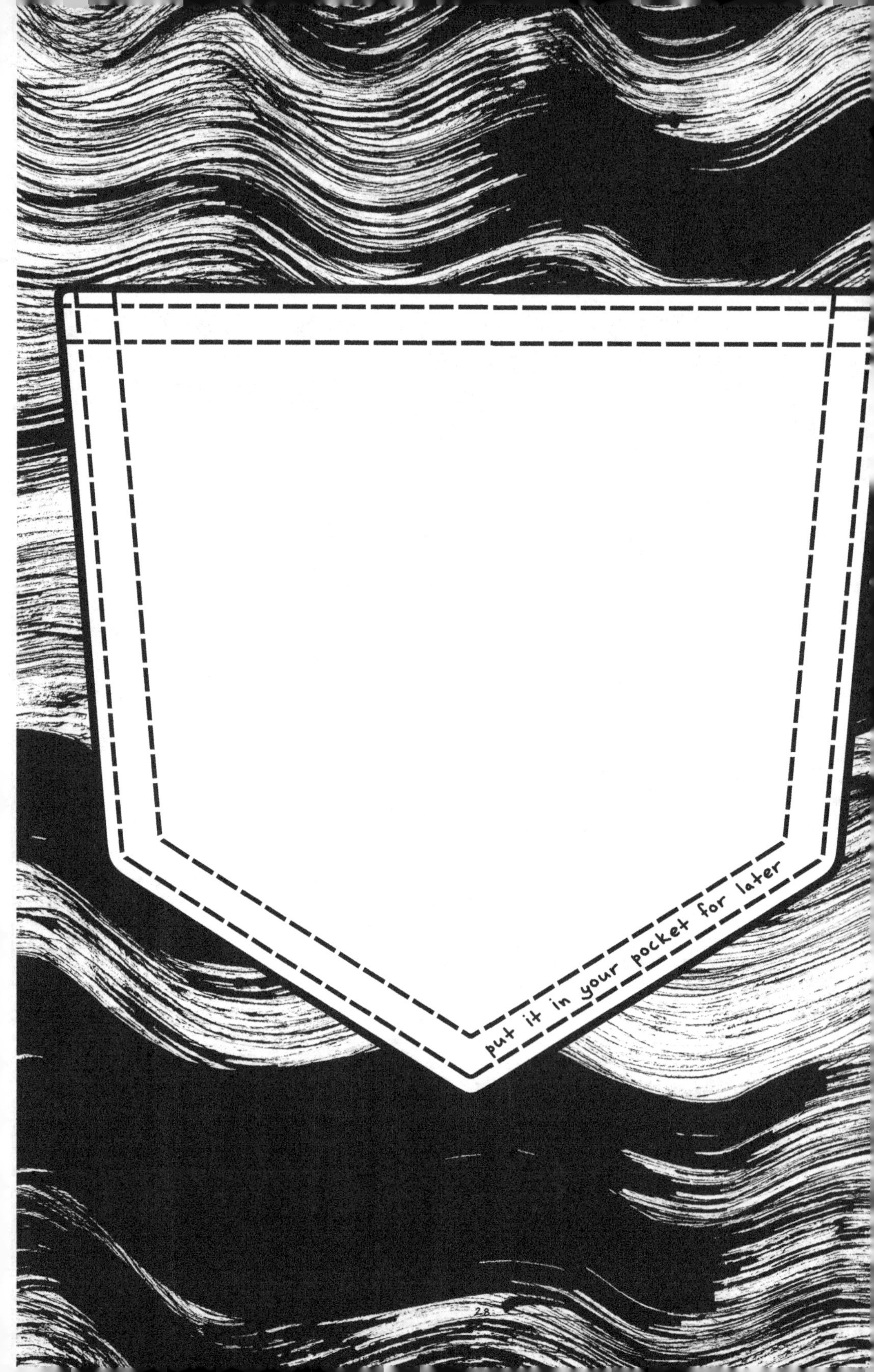

put it in your pocket for later

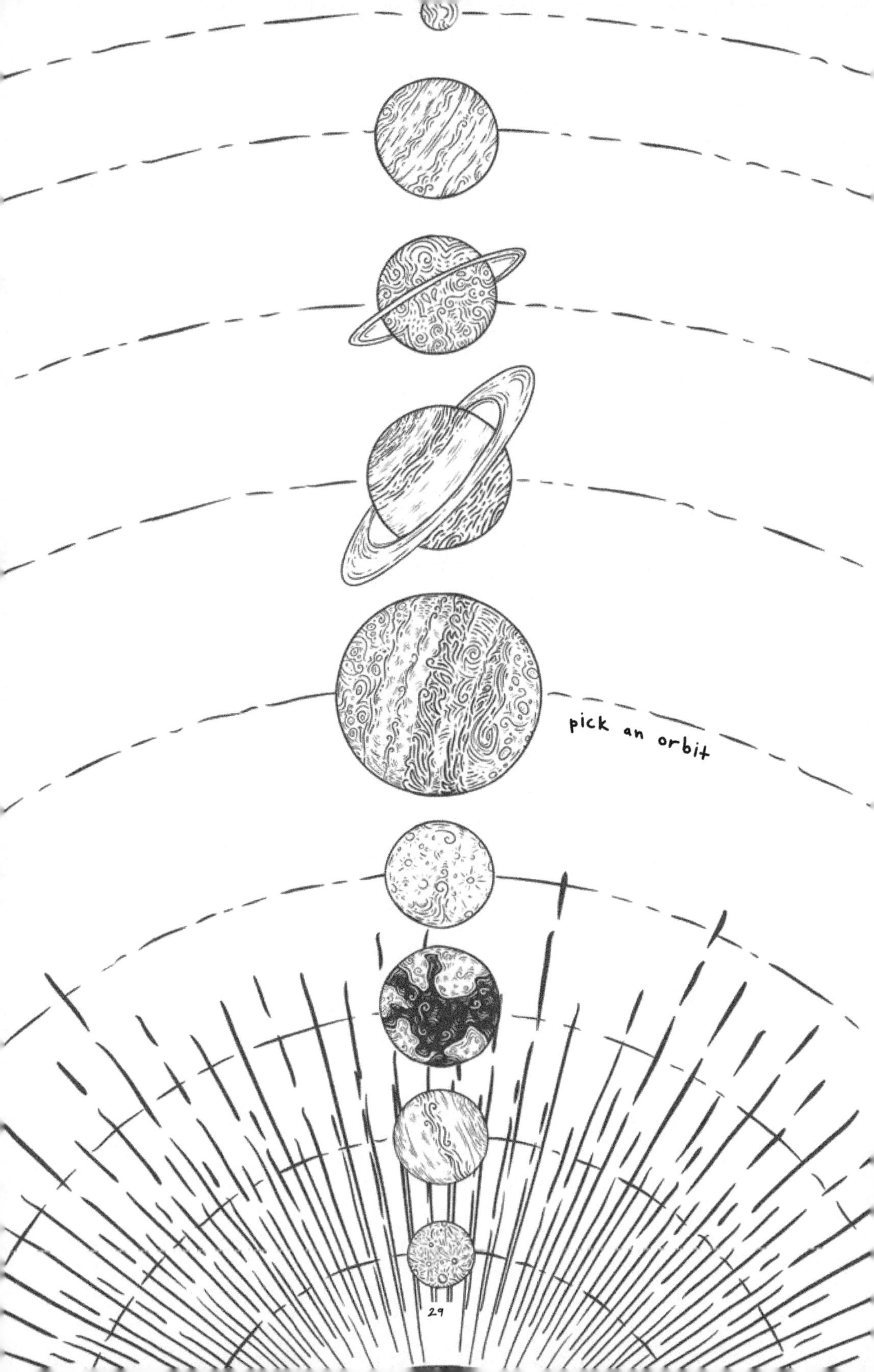
pick an orbit

float an idea

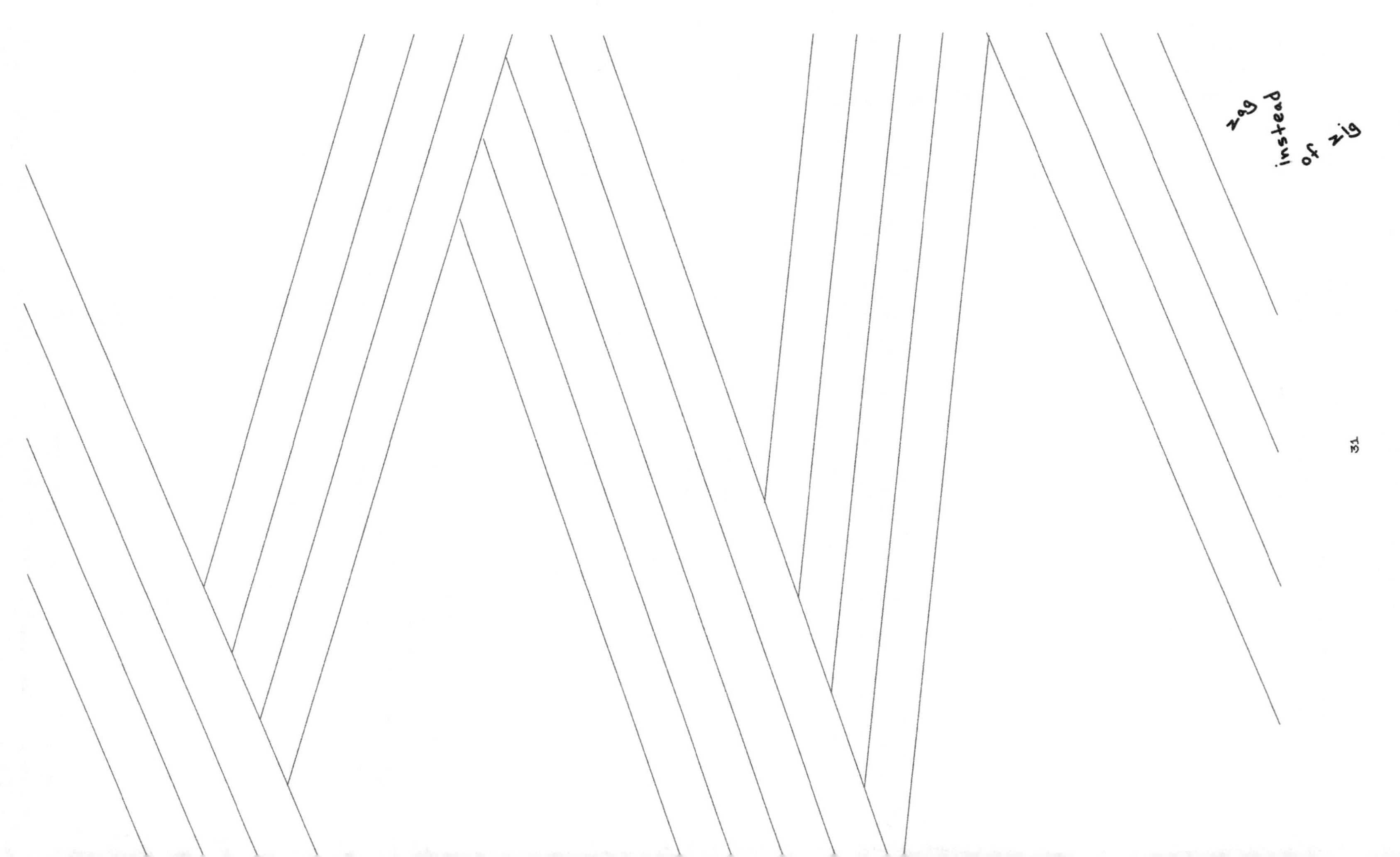

zag
instead
of zig

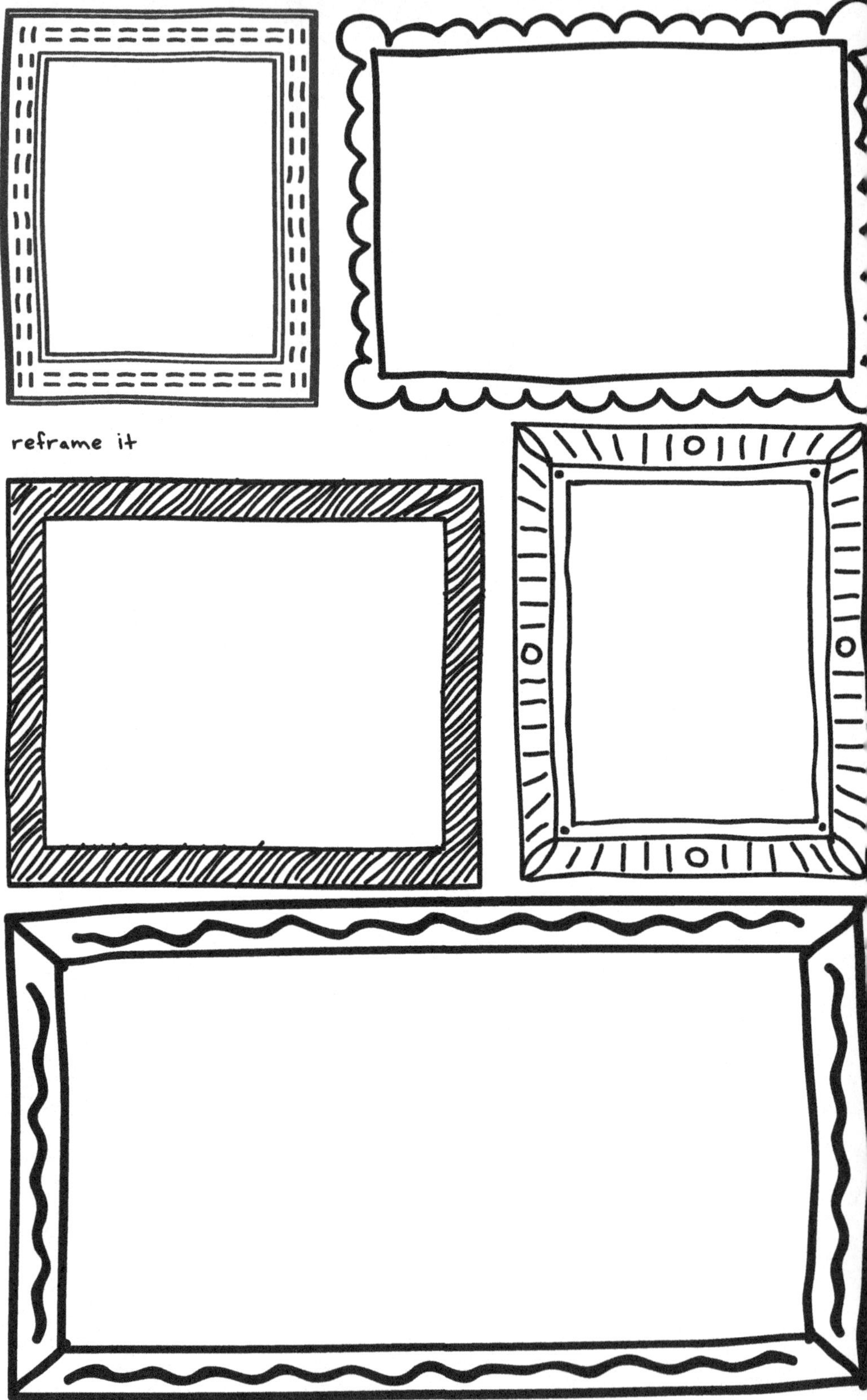
reframe it

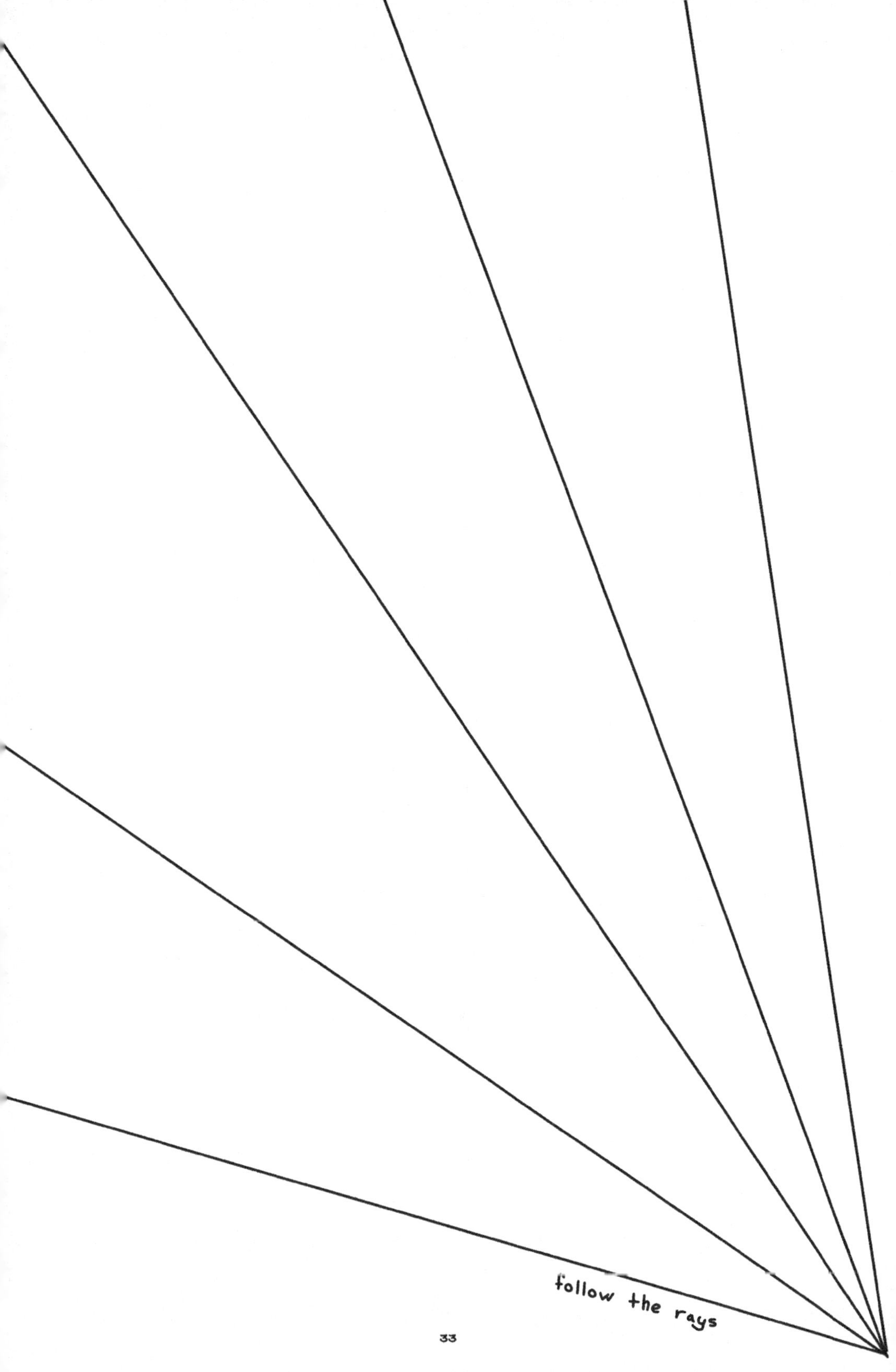

follow the rays

tilt
your
brain

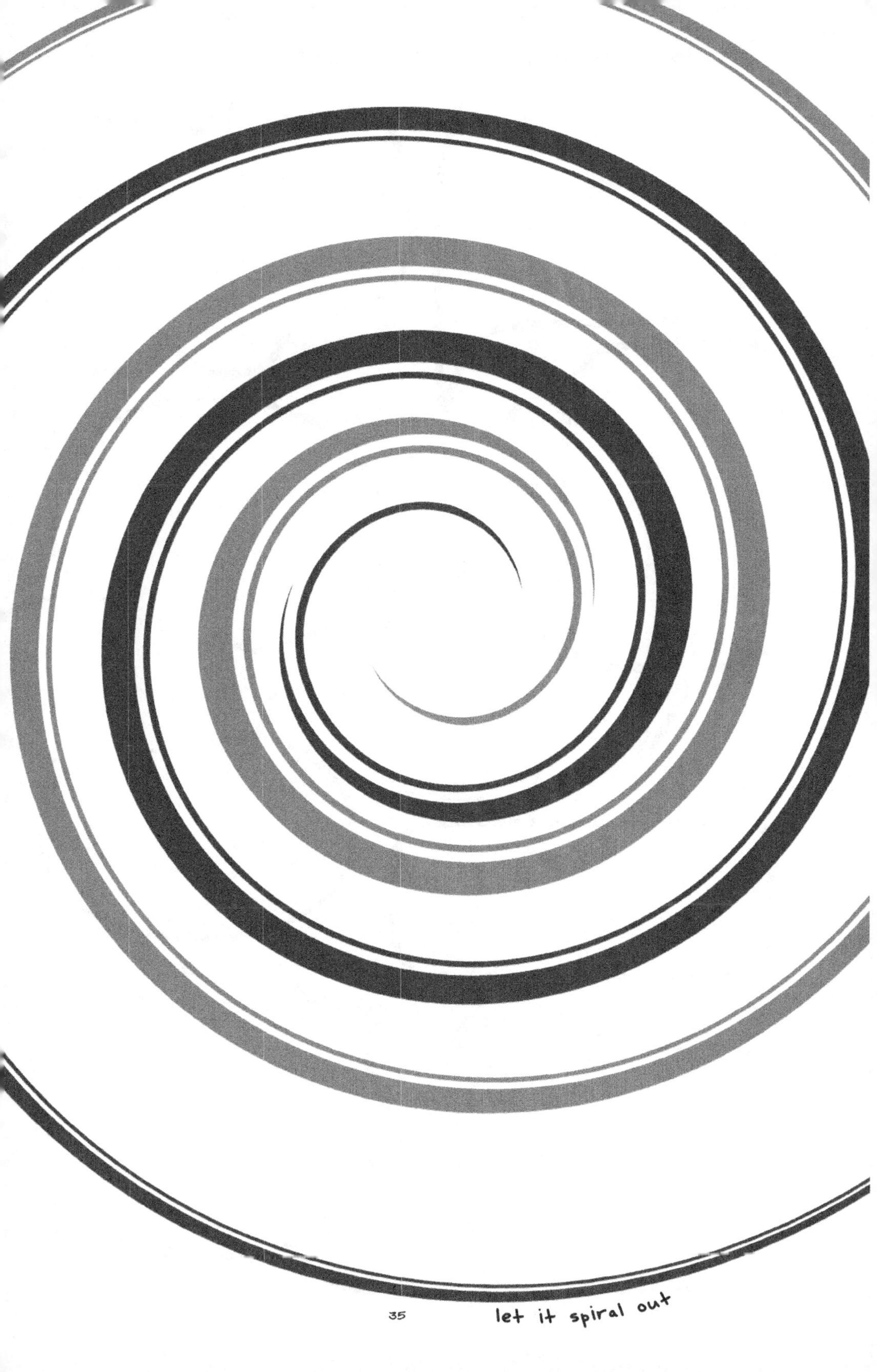

let it spiral out

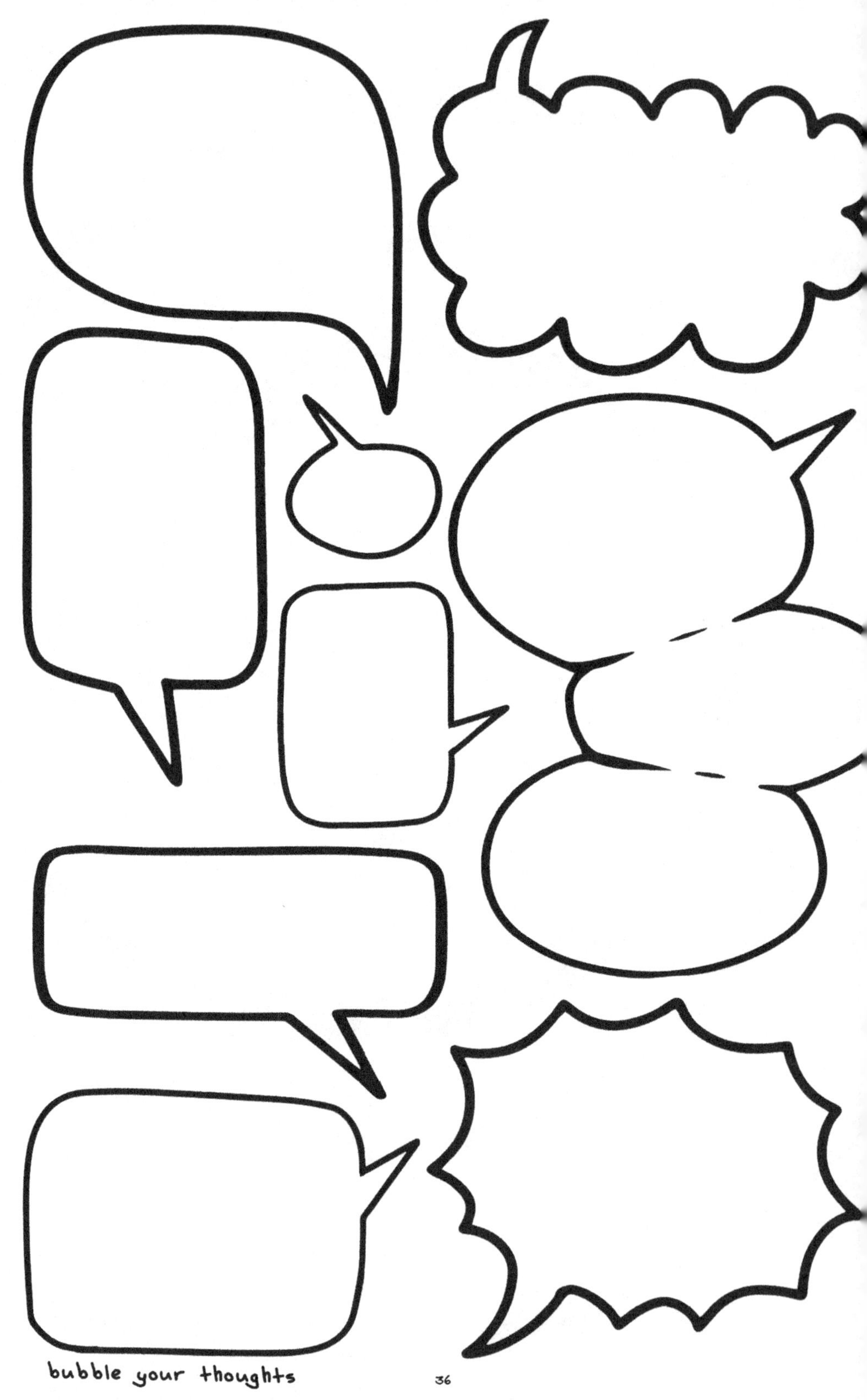

bubble your thoughts

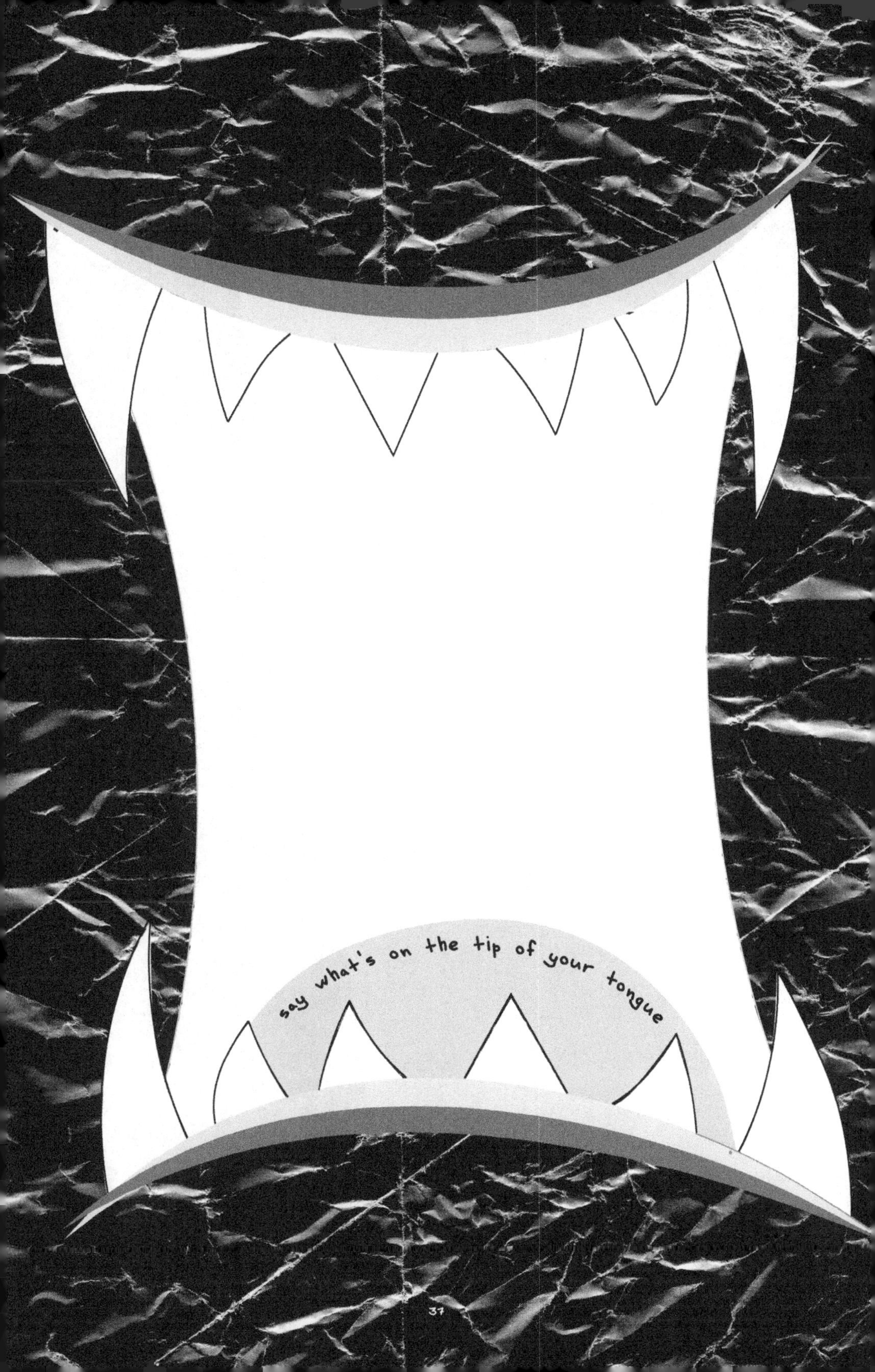
say what's on the tip of your tongue

shine a light on it
38

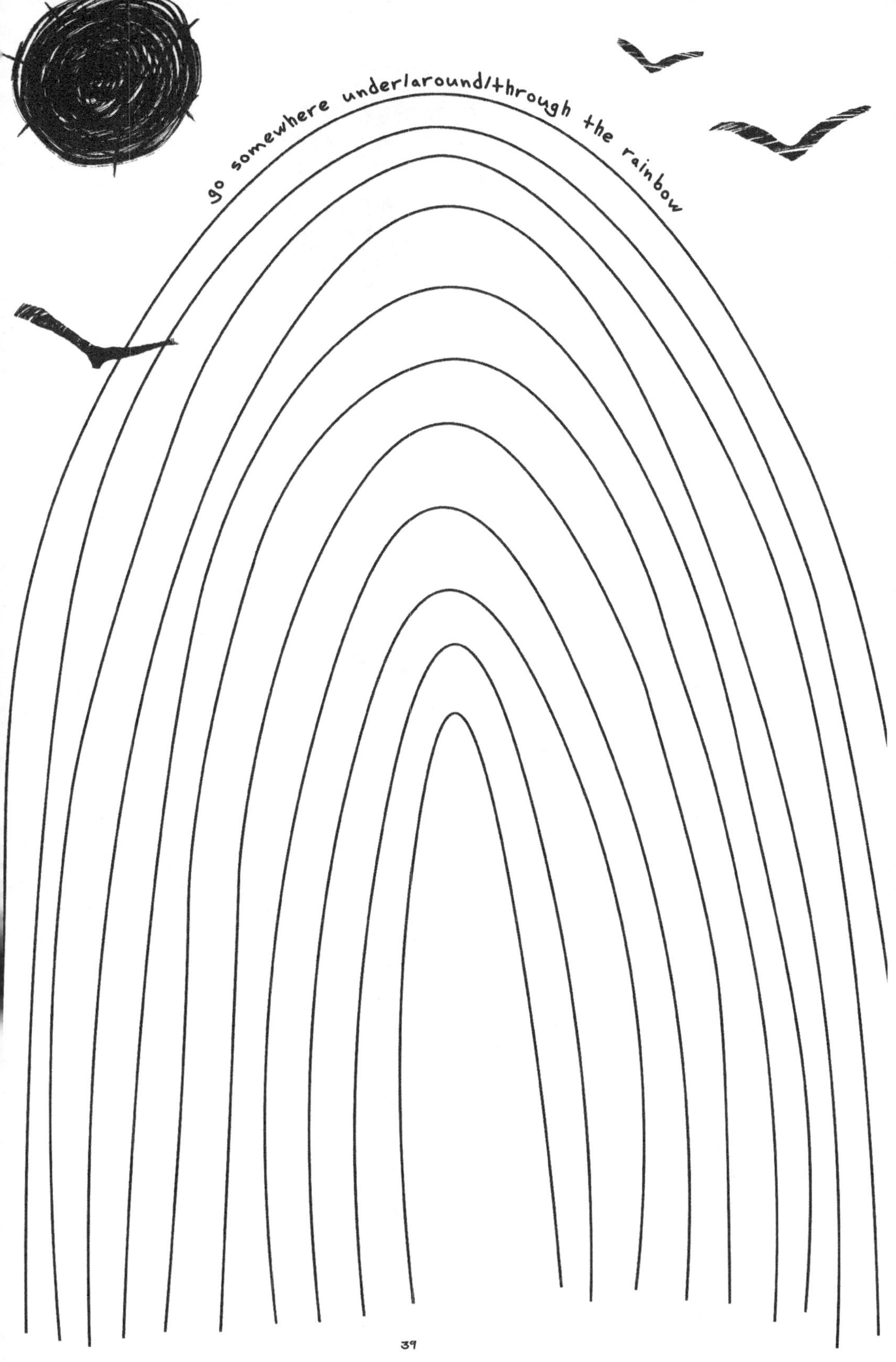

go somewhere under/around/through the rainbow

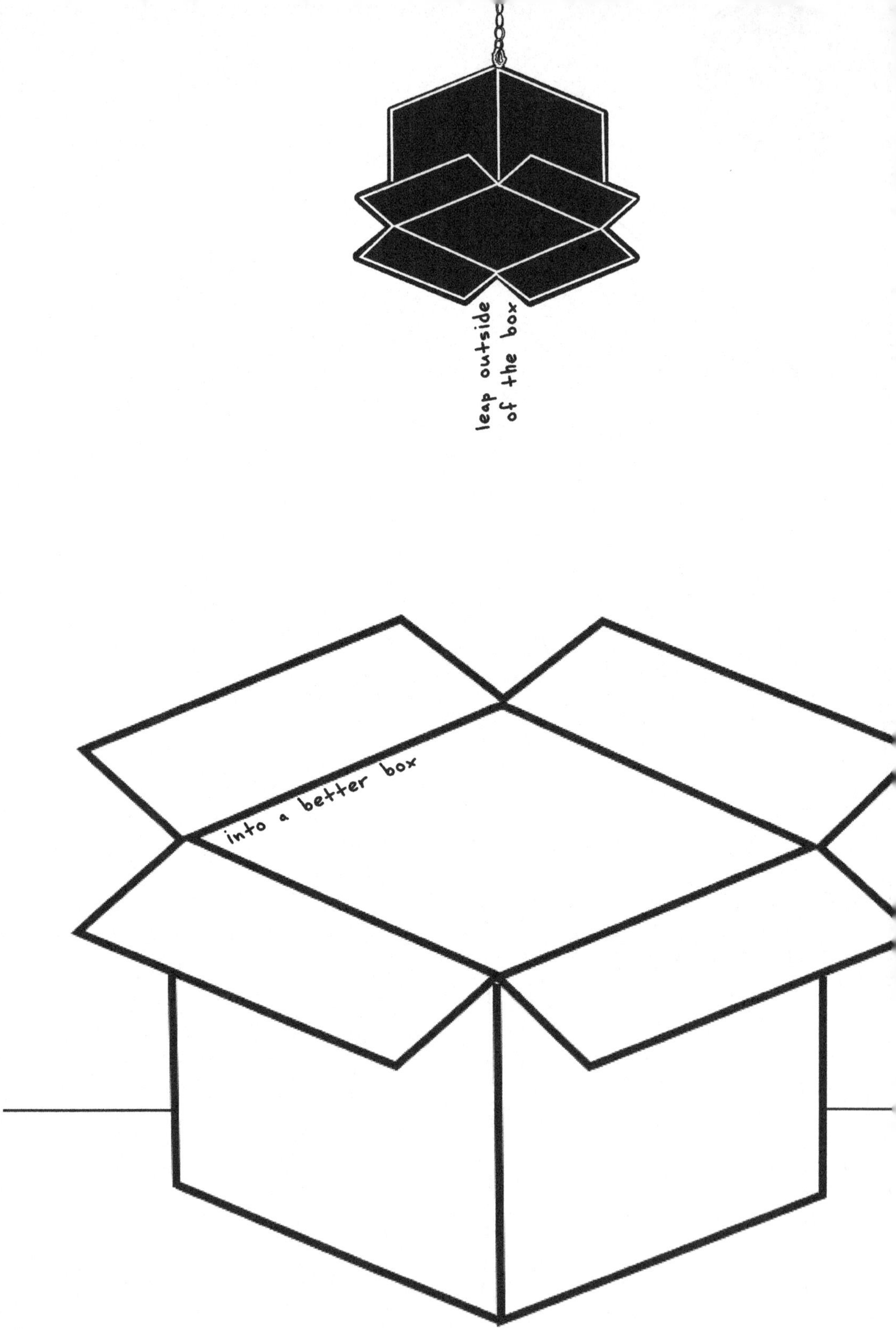

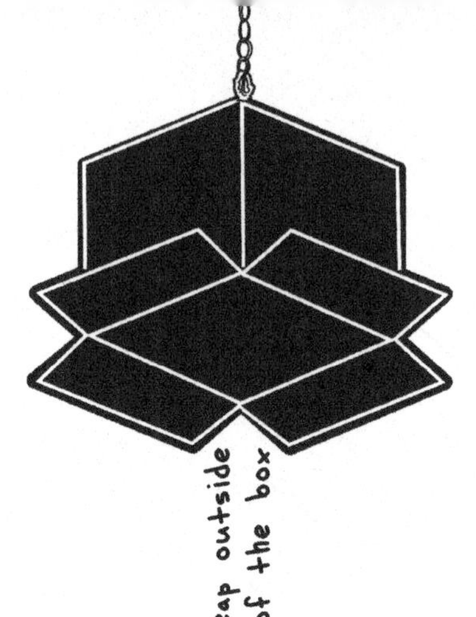

leap outside
of the box

into a better box

write yourself out of a corner

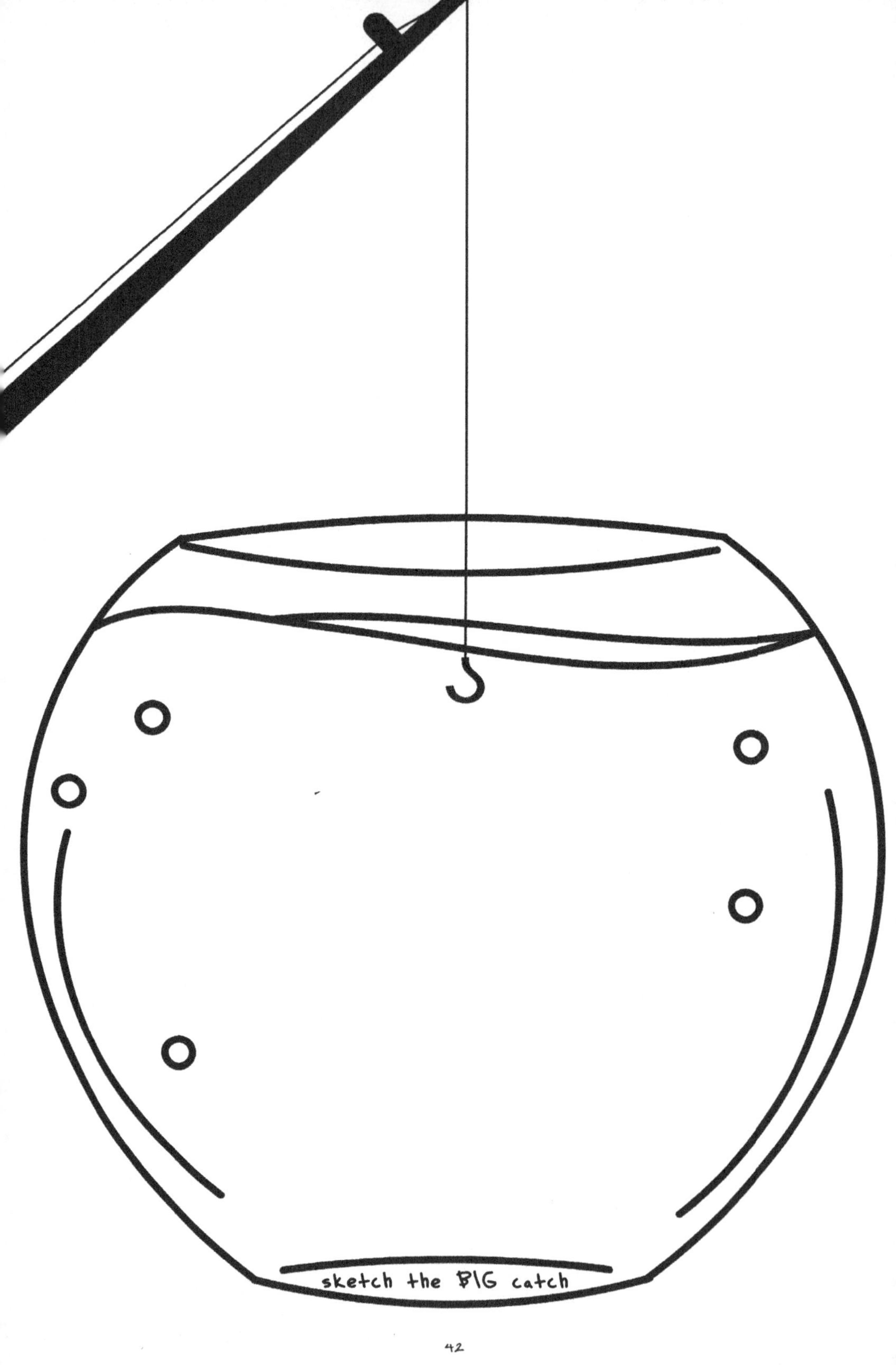

sketch the BIG catch

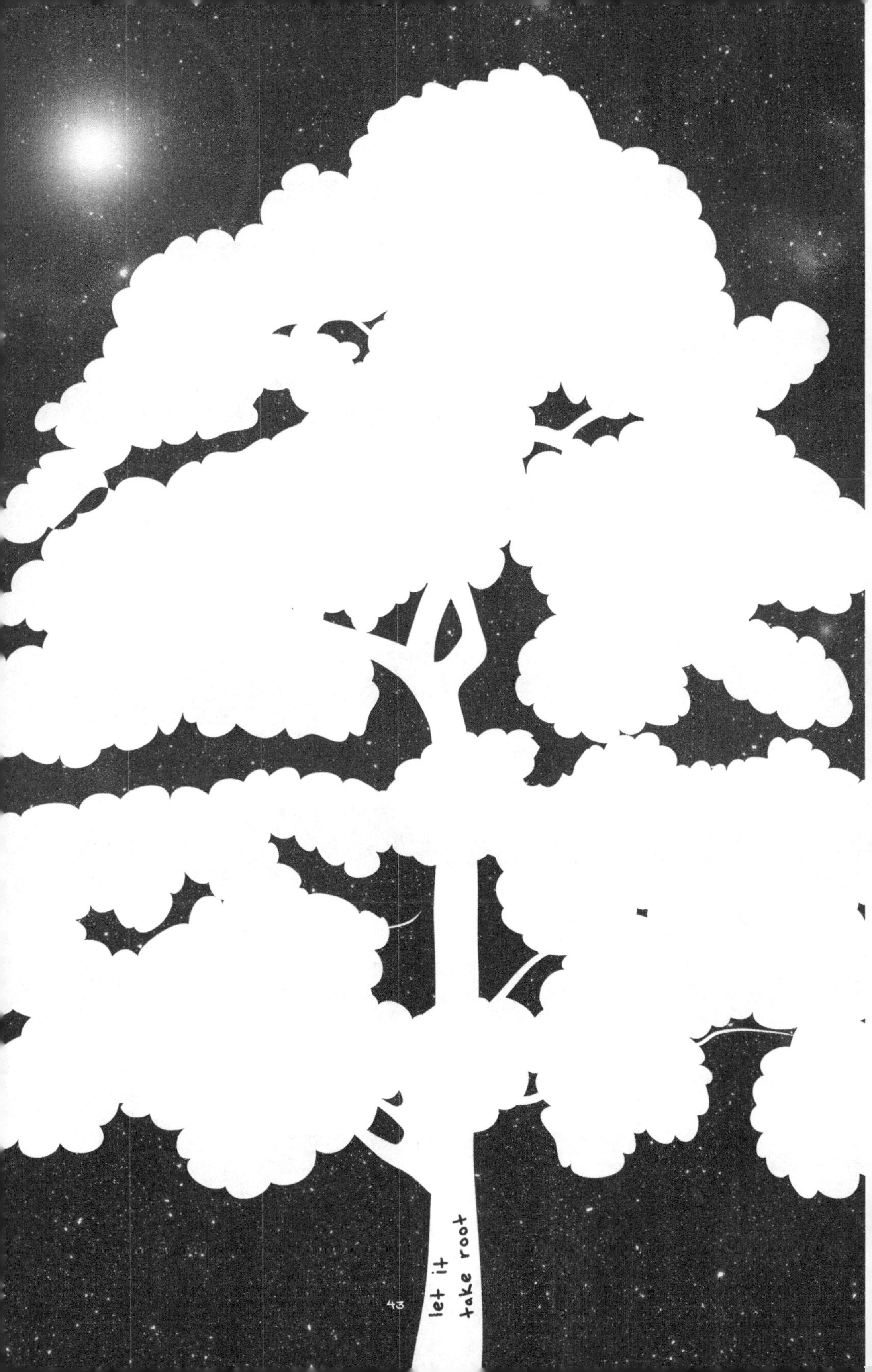

let it
take root

un-redact it
un-redact it
44

turn it upside down

negate the scribbles

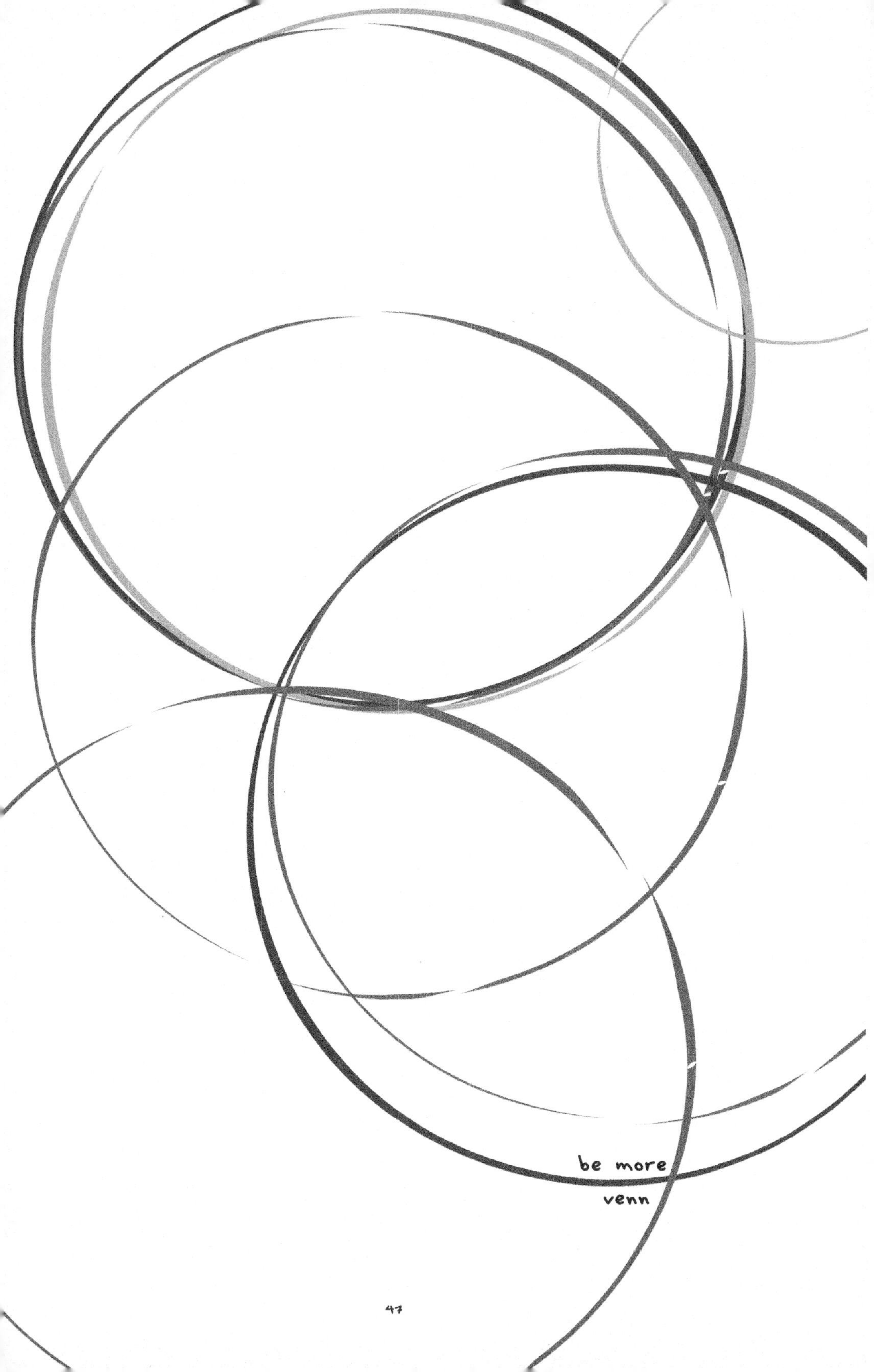
be more
venn

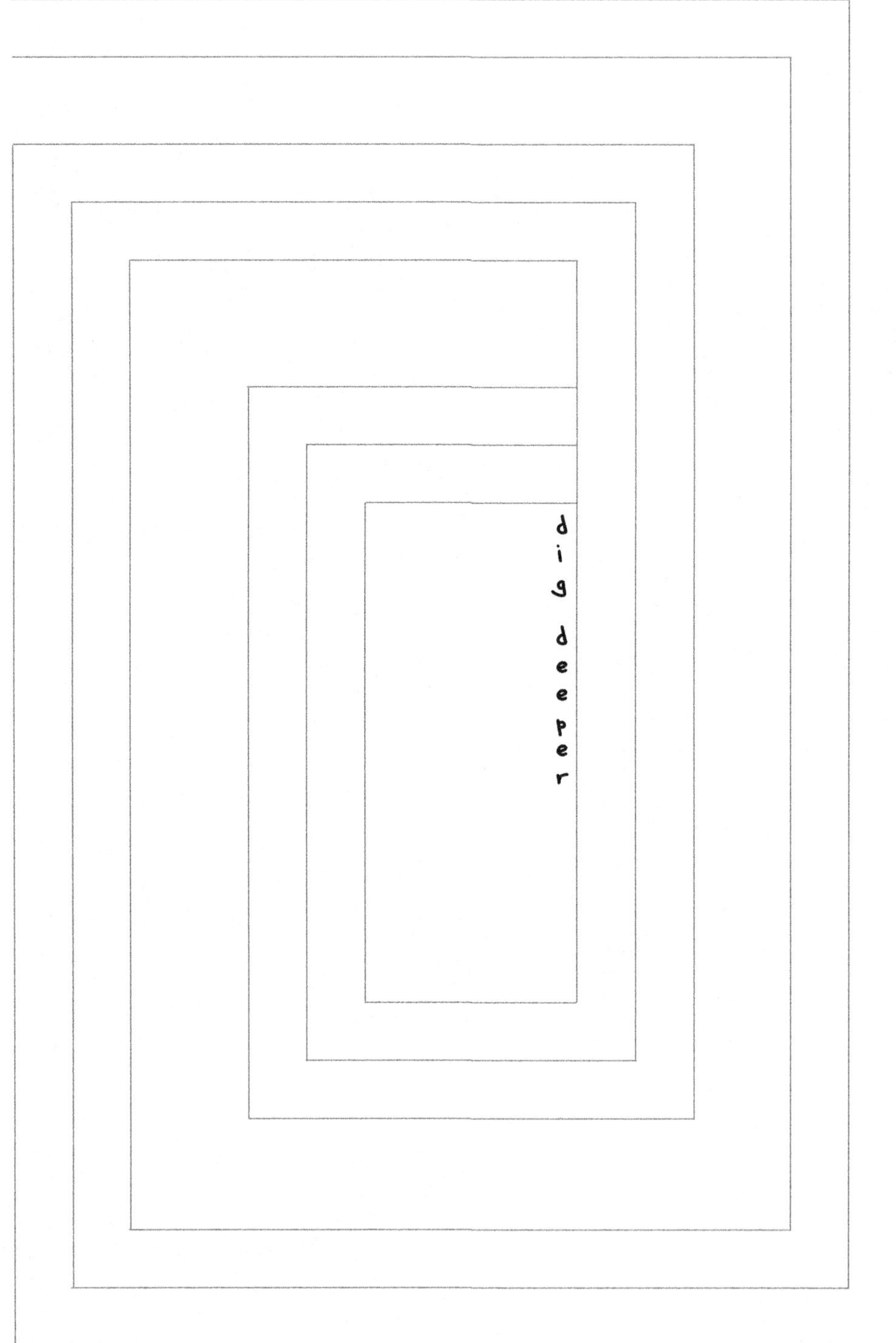

dig deeper

have a proper
brainstorm

vandalize it

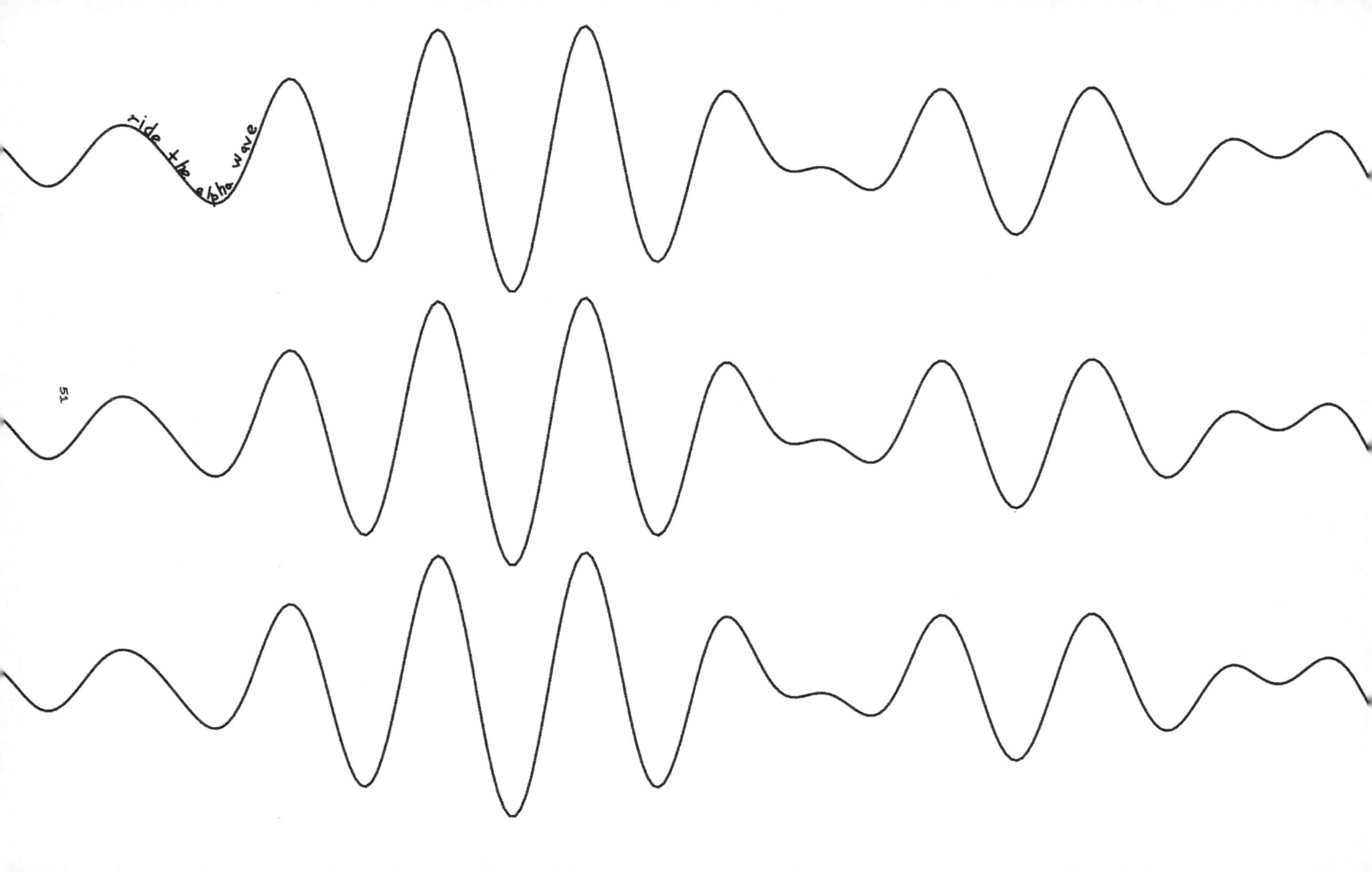
ride the alpha wave

set
it on
fire

SAY.BLURT.SPILLIT.TELL.BEG.SCREAM.UTTER.PROCLAIM.EXPRESS.SPEAK.SHOUT.WHISPER.SPEW.AIRIT.YELL.CRYOUT.EXPLAIN.HOLLER.ECHO.BLARE.VOCALIZE.SPITITOUT.

STATE.PLEAD.BLABBER.MOUTH.COMMENT.SPOUT.REWORD.VENT.VOICE.DISCUSS.ARTICULATE.MUMBLE.SPIN.COMMENT.BLABBER.SAY.BLURT.REWORD.SPILLIT.ARTICULATE.TELL.

ANNOUNCE.BEG.SNARL.SCREAM.ELABORATE.UTTER.PROCLAIM.VENT.EXPRESS.SPEAK.SPOUT.STATE.SHOUT.WHISPER.SPEW.PLEAD.AIR.YELL.CRYOUT.EXPLAIN.DECLARE.HOLLER.

DISCUSS.ECHO.BLARE.VOCALIZE.SPITITOUT.MOUTH.VOICE.ADMIT.SAY.BLURT.SPILLIT.TELL.BEG.SCREAM.UTTER.PROCLAIM.EXPRESS.SPEAK.SHOUT.WHISPER.SPEW.AIRIT.

YELL.CRYOUT.EXPLAIN.HOLLER.ECHO.BLARE.VOCALIZE.SPITITOUT.STATE.PLEAD.BLABBER.MOUTH.COMMENT.SPOUT.REWORD.VENT.VOICE.DISCUSS.ARTICULATE.MUMBLE.SPIN.

COMMENT.BLABBER.SAY.BLURT.REWORD.SPILLIT.ARTICULATE.TELL.ANNOUNCE.BEG.ADMIT.SNARL.SCREAM.ELABORATE.UTTER.PROCLAIM.VENT.EXPRESS.SPEAK.SPOUT.STATE.

SHOUT.WHISPER.SPEW.PLEAD.AIR.YELL.CRYOUT.EXPLAIN.DECLARE.HOLLER.DISCUSS.ECHO.BLARE.VOCALIZE.SPITITOUT.MOUTH.VOICE.SAY.BLURT.SPILLIT.TELL.BEG.SCREAM.

UTTER.PROCLAIM.EXPRESS.SPEAK.SHOUT.WHISPER.SPEW.AIRIT.YELL.CRYOUT.EXPLAIN.HOLLER.ECHO.BLARE.VOCALIZE.SPITITOUT.STATE.PLEAD.BLABBER.MOUTH.COMMENT.SPOUT.

REWORD.VENT.VOICE.DISCUSS.ARTICULATE.ADMIT.MUMBLE.SPIN.COMMENT.BLABBER.SAY.BLURT.REWORD.SPILLIT.ARTICULATE.TELL.ANNOUNCE.BEG.SNARL.SCREAM.ELABORATE.

UTTER.PROCLAIM.VENT.EXPRESS.SPEAK.SPOUT.STATE.SHOUT.WHISPER.SPEW.PLEAD.AIR.YELL.CRYOUT.EXPLAIN.DECLARE.HOLLER.DISCUSS.ECHO.BLARE.VOCALIZE.SPITITOUT.

MOUTH.VOICE.SAY.BLURT.SPILLIT.TELL.BEG.SCREAM.UTTER.PROCLAIM.EXPRESS.SPEAK.SHOUT.WHISPER.SPEW.AIRIT.YELL.CRYOUT.EXPLAIN.HOLLER.ECHO.BLARE.

VOCALIZE.SPITITOUT.STATE.PLEAD.BLABBER.MOUTH.COMMENT.SPOUT.REWORD.VENT.VOICE.DISCUSS.ARTICULATE.MUMBLE.SPIN.COMMENT.BLABBER.SAY.BLURT.REWORD.SPILLIT.

ARTICULATE.TELL.ANNOUNCE.BEG.SNARL.SCREAM.ELABORATE.UTTER.PROCLAIM.VENT.EXPRESS.SPEAK.SPOUT.STATE.SHOUT.WHISPER.SPEW.PLEAD.AIR.YELL.CRYOUT.

EXPLAIN.DECLARE.HOLLER.DISCUSS.ECHO.BLARE.VOCALIZE.SPITITOUT.MOUTH.VOICE.SAY.BLURT.SPILLIT.SUGGEST.TELL.BEG.SCREAM.UTTER.PROCLAIM.EXPRESS.SPEAK.SHOUT.

WHISPER.SPEW.AIRIT.YELL.CRYOUT.EXPLAIN.HOLLER.ECHO.BLARE.VOCALIZE.SPITITOUT.STATE.PLEAD.BLABBER.MOUTH.COMMENT.SPOUT.REWORD.VENT.VOICE.DISCUSS.

ARTICULATE.MUMBLE.SPIN.COMMENT.BLABBER.SAY.BLURT.REWORD.SPILLIT.ARTICULATE.TELL.ANNOUNCE.BEG.SNARL.SCREAM.ELABORATE.UTTER.PROCLAIM.VENT.EXPRESS.SPEAK.

SPOUT.STATE.SHOUT.WHISPER.SPEW.PLEAD.AIR.YELL.CRYOUT.EXPLAIN.DECLARE.HOLLER.DISCUSS.ECHO.BLARE.VOCALIZE.SPITITOUT.MOUTH.VOICE.SAY.BLURT.SPILLIT.

TELL.BEG.SCREAM.UTTER.PROCLAIM.EXPRESS.SUGGEST.SPEAK.SHOUT.WHISPER.SPEW.AIRIT.YELL.CRYOUT.EXPLAIN.HOLLER.ECHO.BLARE.VOCALIZE.SPITITOUT.STATE.PLEAD.

BLABBER.ADMIT.MOUTH.COMMENT.SPOUT.REWORD.VENT.VOICE.DISCUSS.ARTICULATE.MUMBLE.SPIN.COMMENT.BLABBER.SAY.BLURT.REWORD.SPILLIT.ARTICULATE.TELL.

ANNOUNCE.BEG.SNARL.SCREAM.ELABORATE.UTTER.PROCLAIM.VENT.EXPRESS.SPEAK.SPOUT.STATE.SHOUT.WHISPER.SPEW.PLEAD.AIR.YELL.CRYOUT.EXPLAIN.SUGGEST.DECLARE.

HOLLER.DISCUSS.ECHO.BLARE.VOCALIZE.SPITITOUT.MOUTH.VOICE.SAY.BLURT.SPILLIT.TELL.BEG.SCREAM.UTTER.PROCLAIM.EXPRESS.SPEAK.SHOUT.WHISPER.SPEW.AIRIT.YELL.

CRYOUT.EXPLAIN.HOLLER.ECHO.ADMIT.BLARE.VOCALIZE.SPITITOUT.STATE.PLEAD.BLABBER.MOUTH.COMMENT.SPOUT.REWORD.VENT.VOICE.DISCUSS.ARTICULATE.MUMBLE.SPIN.

COMMENT.BLABBER.SAY.BLURT.REWORD.SPILLIT.ARTICULATE.TELL.ANNOUNCE.BEG.SNARL.SCREAM.ELABORATE.UTTER.PROCLAIM.VENT.EXPRESS.SPEAK.SPOUT.STATE.SHOUT.

WHISPER.ADMIT.SPEW.PLEAD.AIR.YELL.CRYOUT.EXPLAIN.DECLARE.HOLLER.DISCUSS.ECHO.BLARE.VOCALIZE.SPITITOUT.MOUTH.VOICE.SAY.BLURT.SPILLIT.TELL.BEG.SCREAM.

UTTER.PROCLAIM.EXPRESS.SPEAK.SHOUT.WHISPER.SPEW.AIRIT.YELL.CRYOUT.EXPLAIN.HOLLER.ECHO.BLARE.VOCALIZE.SPITITOUT.STATE.PLEAD.BLABBER.MOUTH.COMMENT.

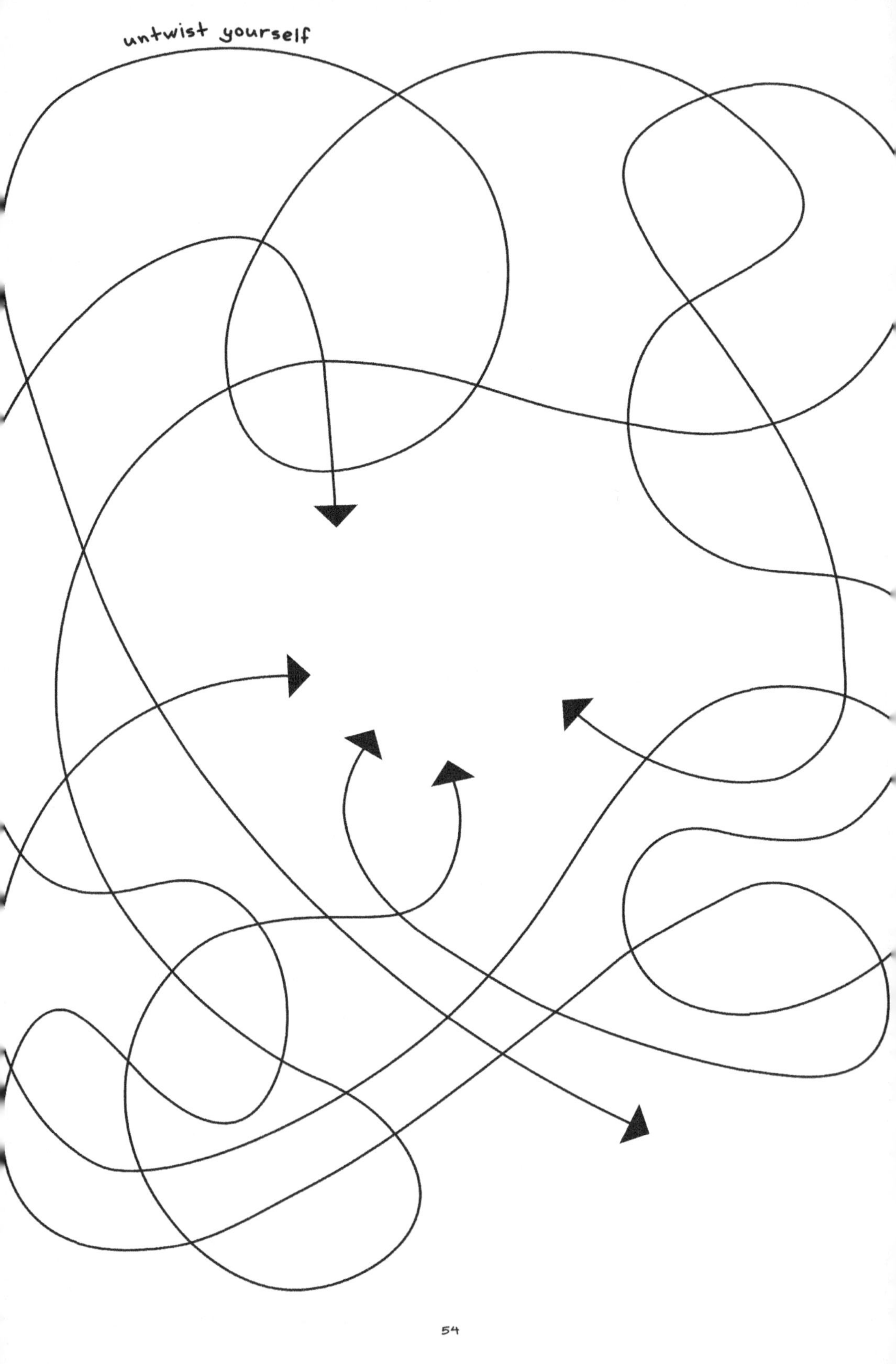
untwist yourself

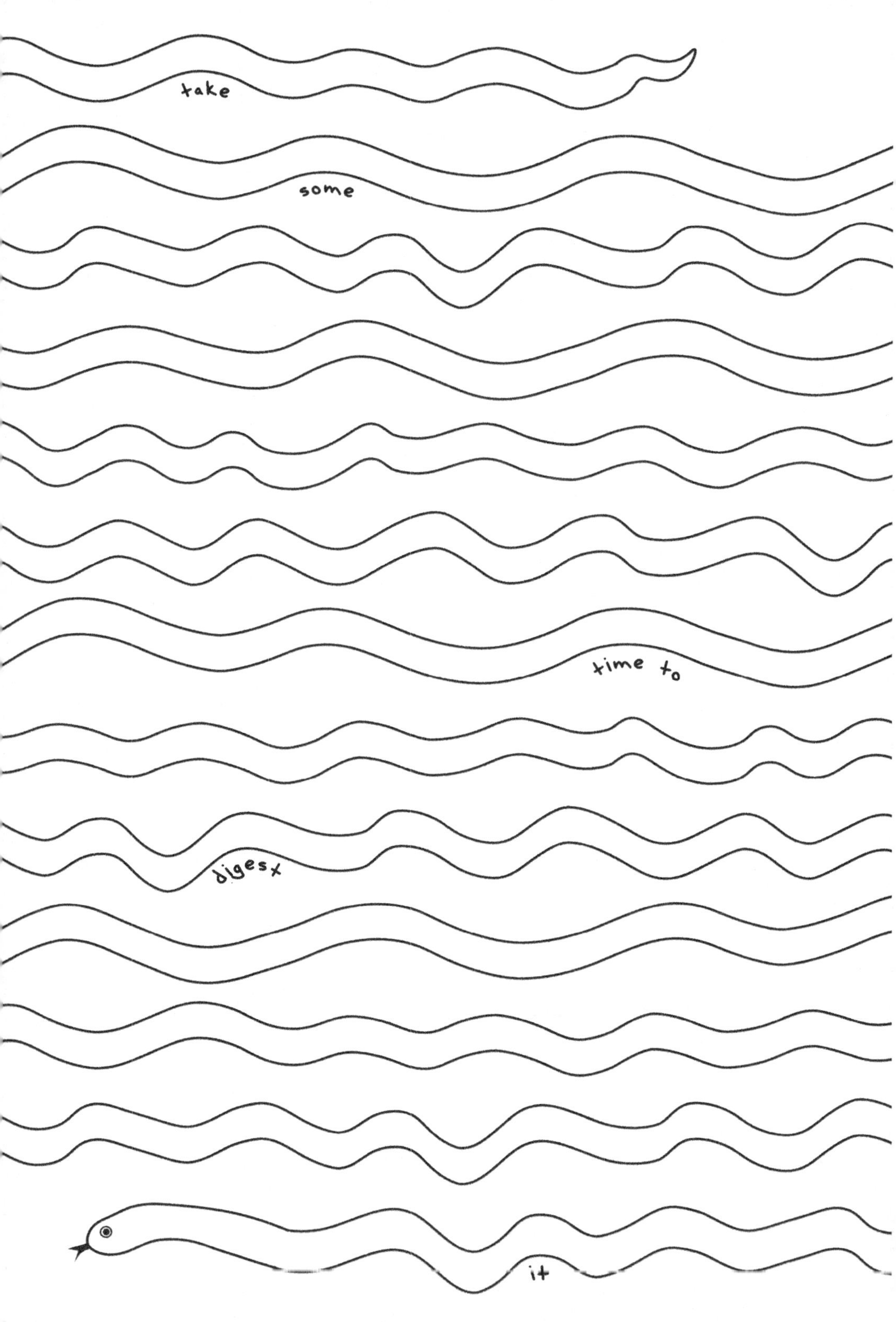
take
some
time to
digest
it

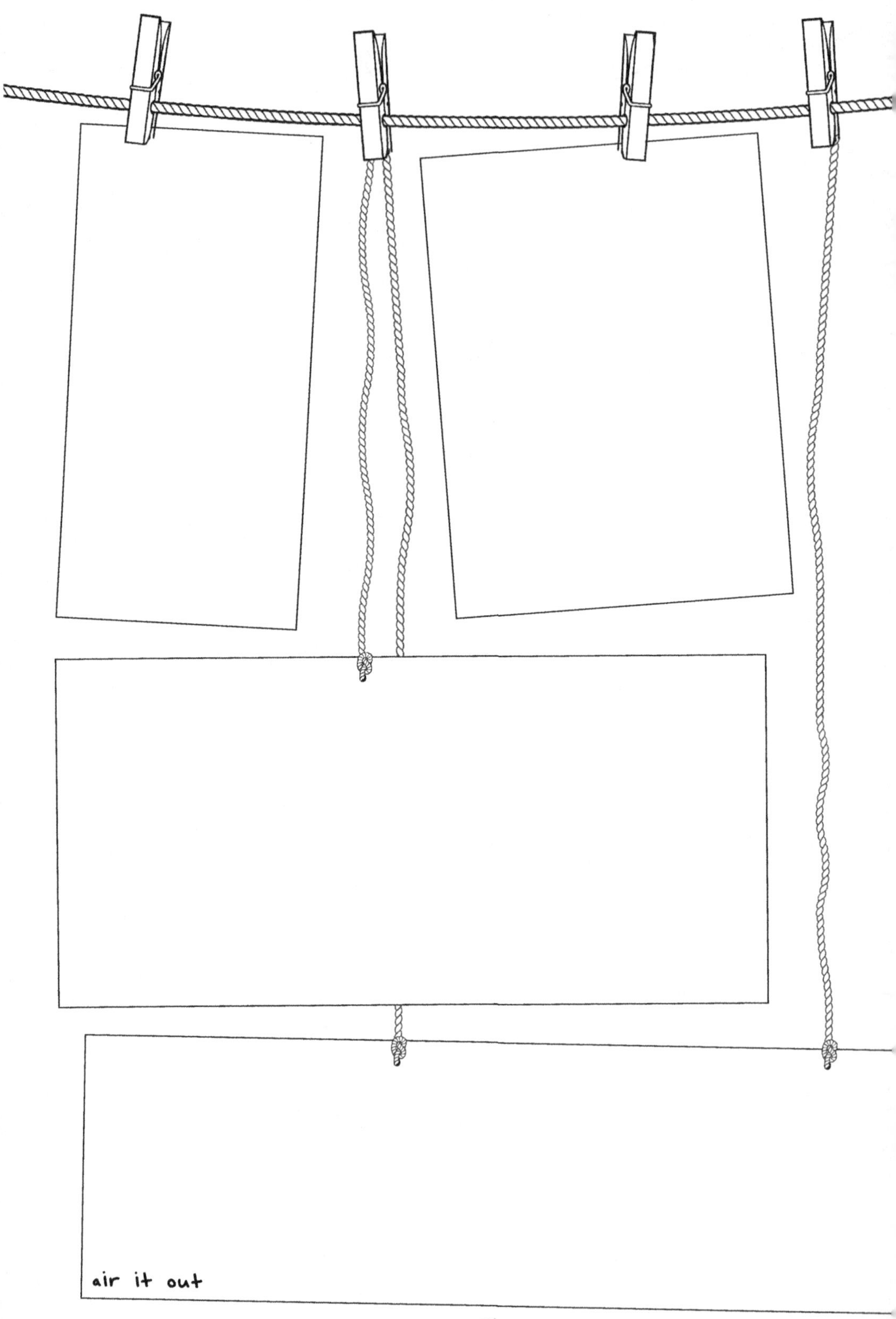
air it out
air it out

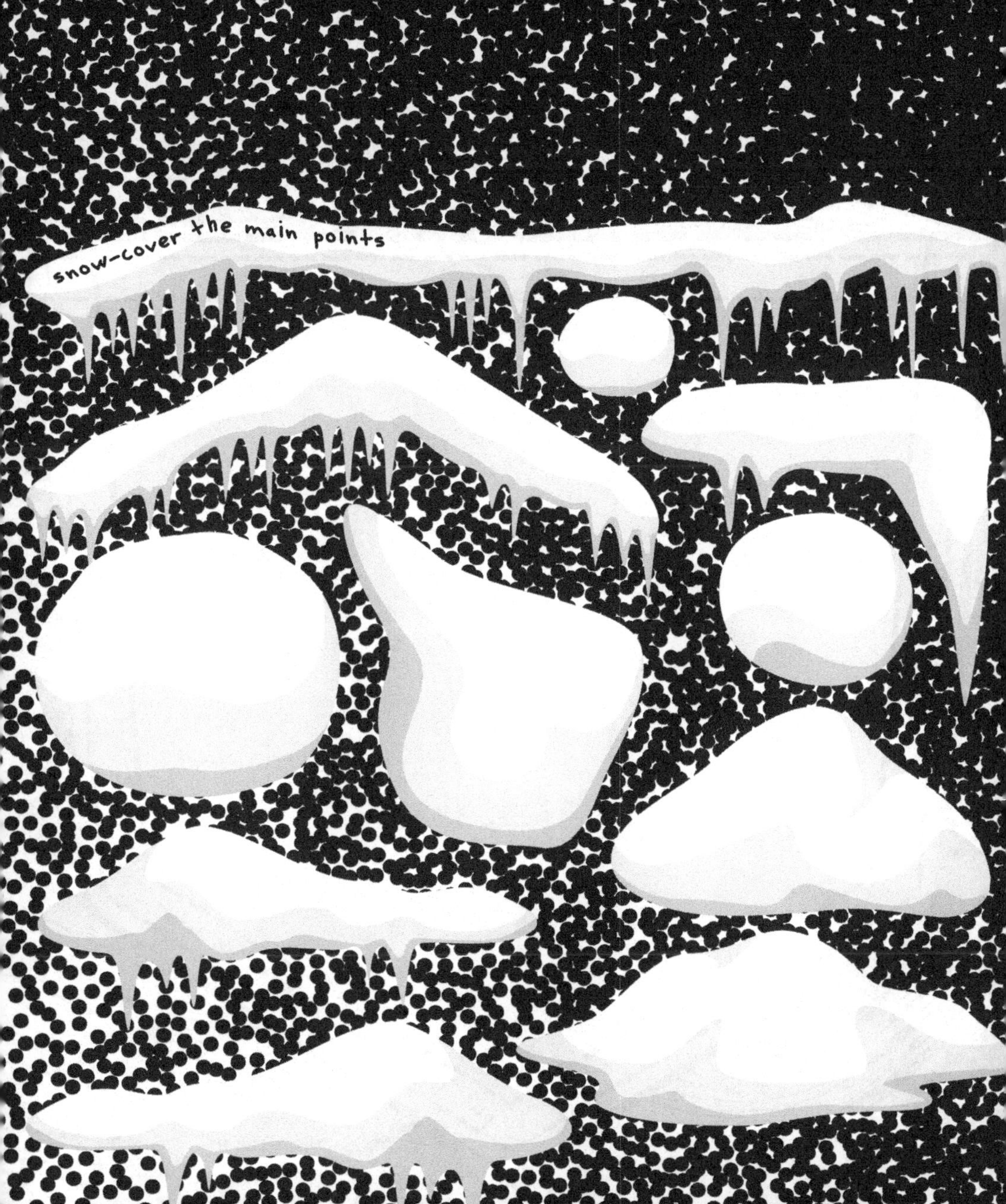

snow-cover the main points

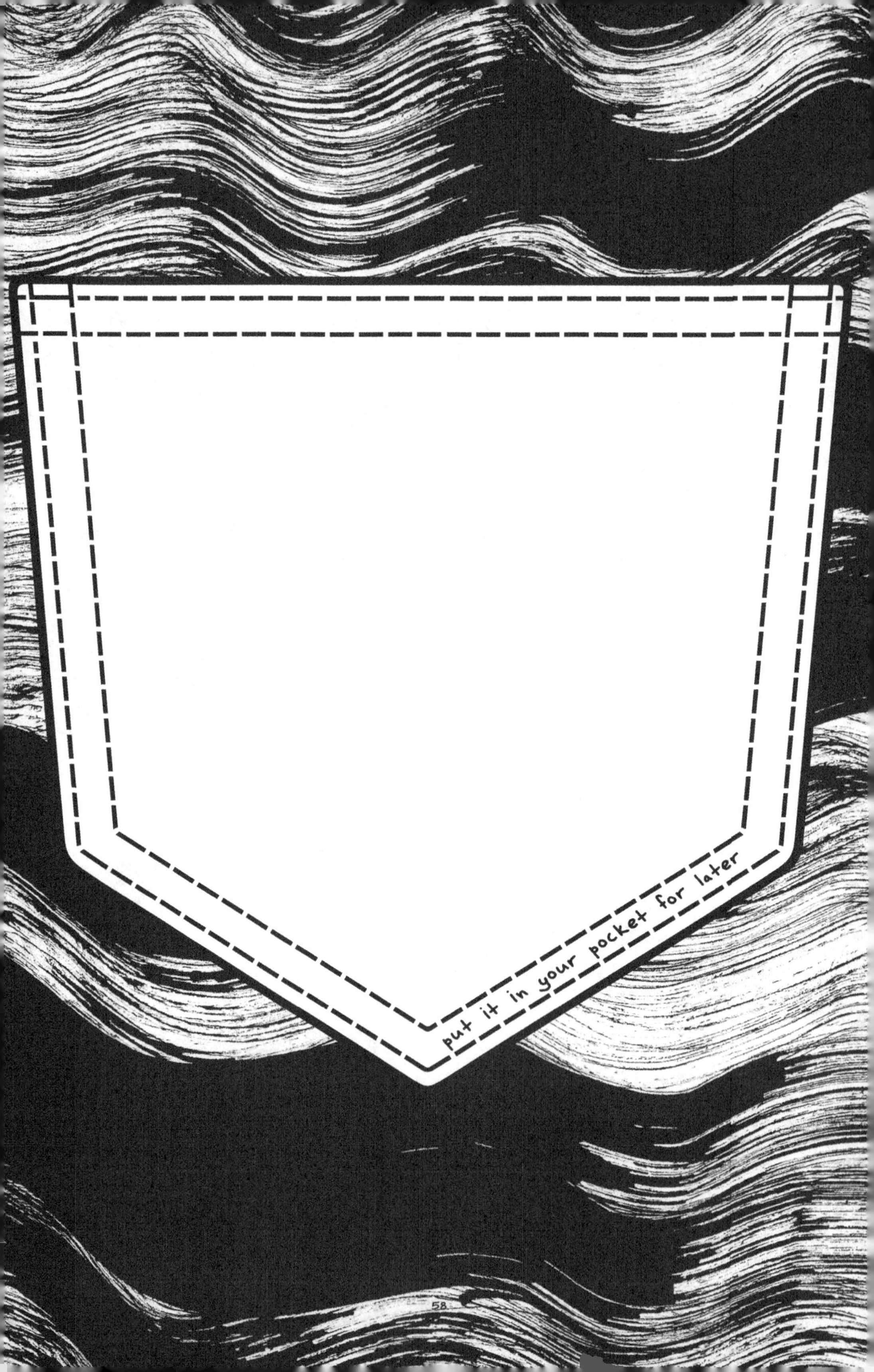
put it in your pocket for later

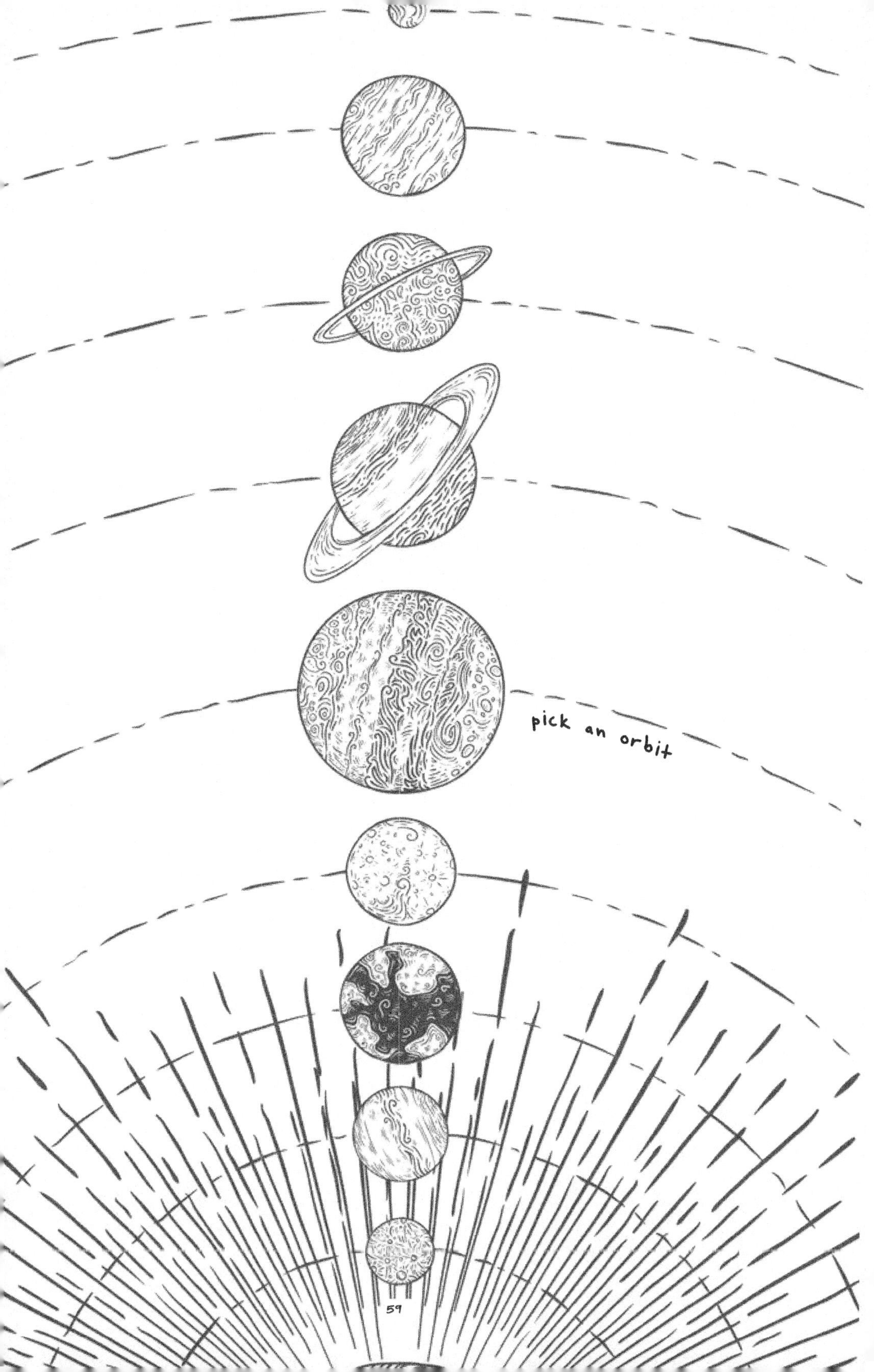
pick an orbit

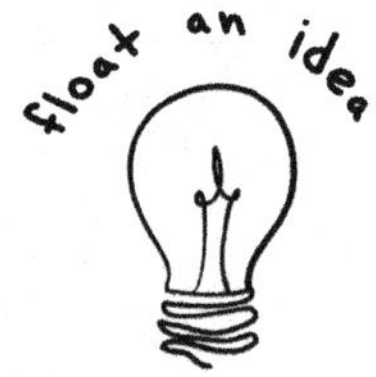

float an idea

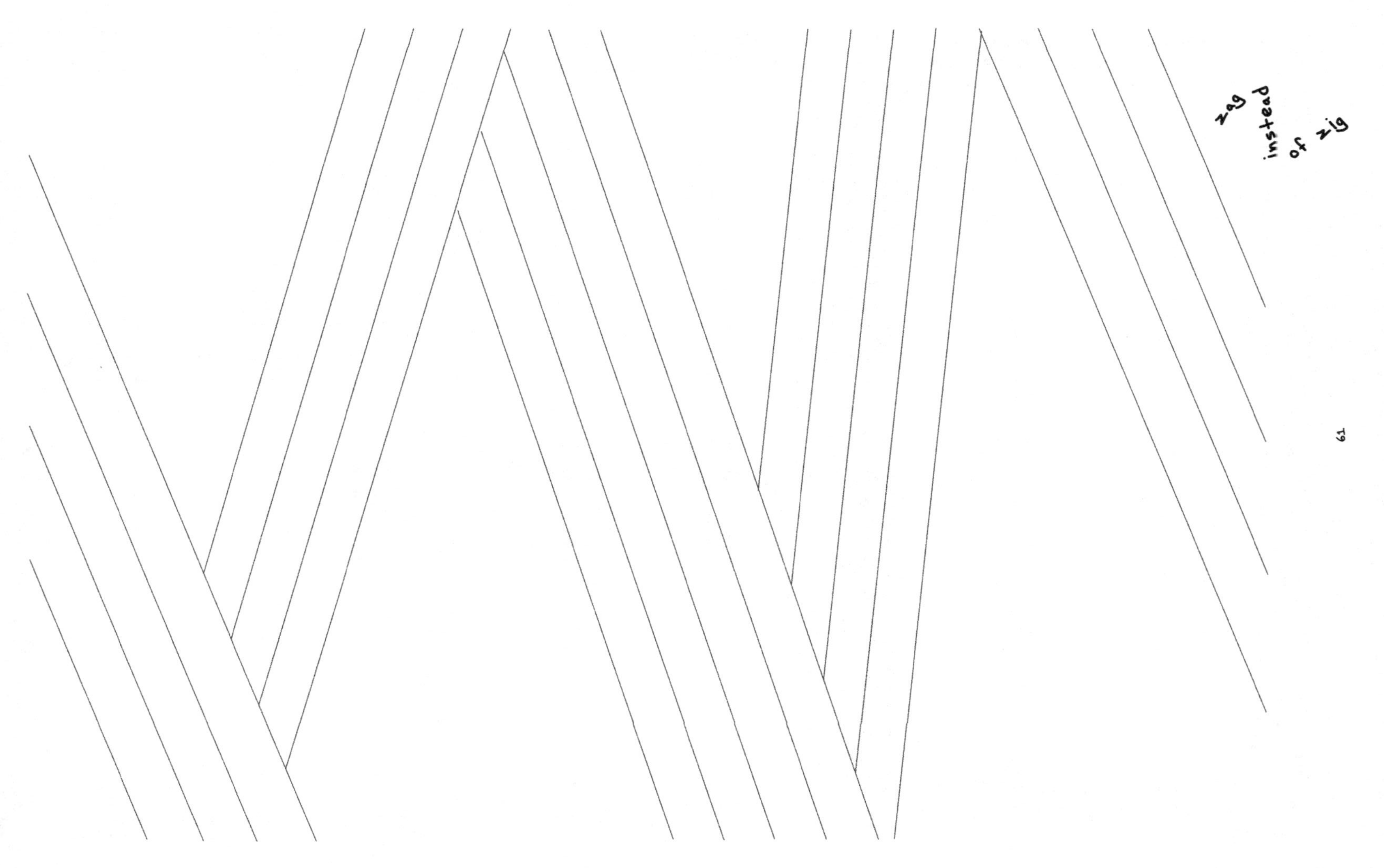

zag
instead
of zig

reframe it

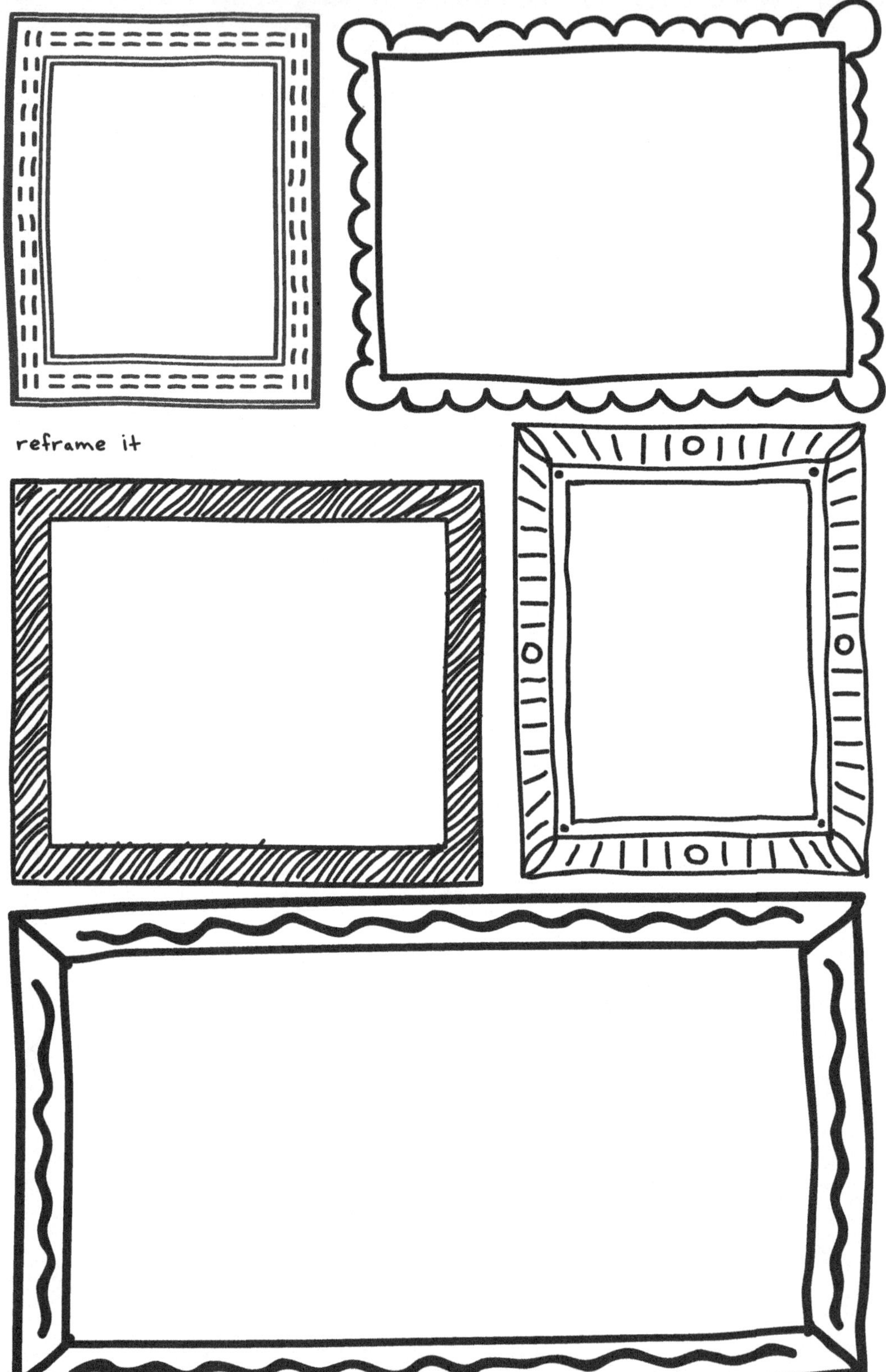

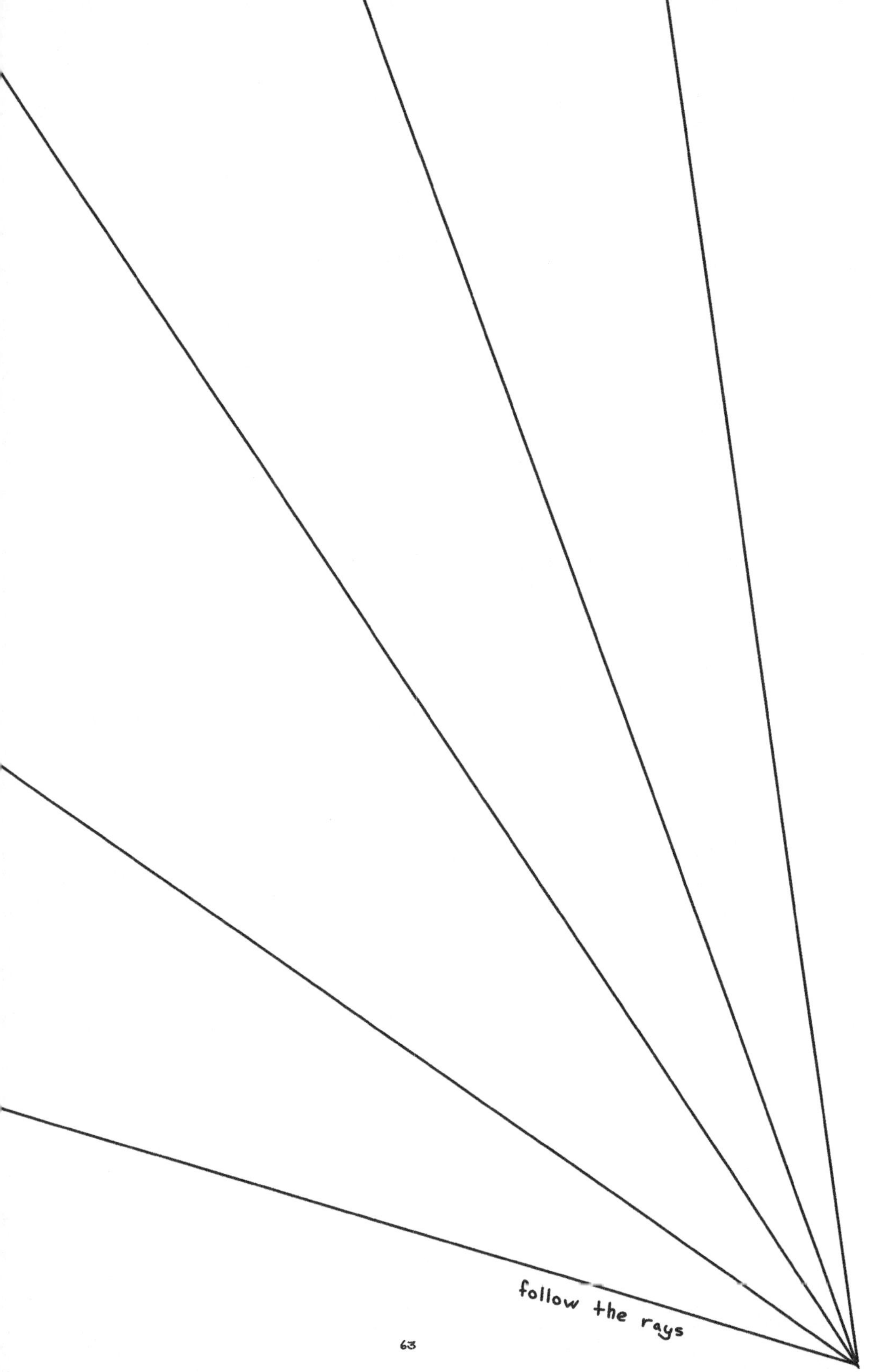

follow the rays

tilt

your

brain

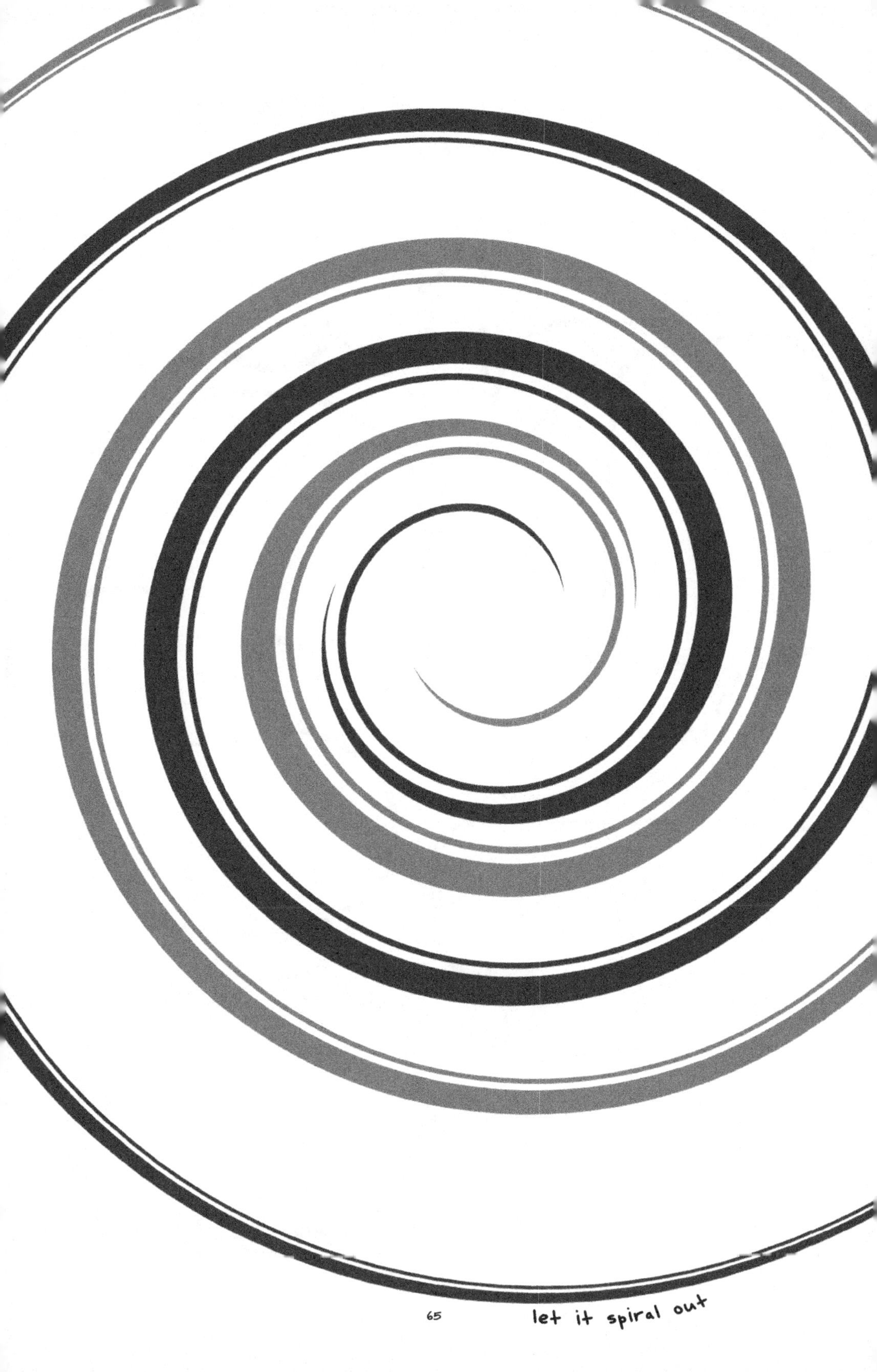
let it spiral out

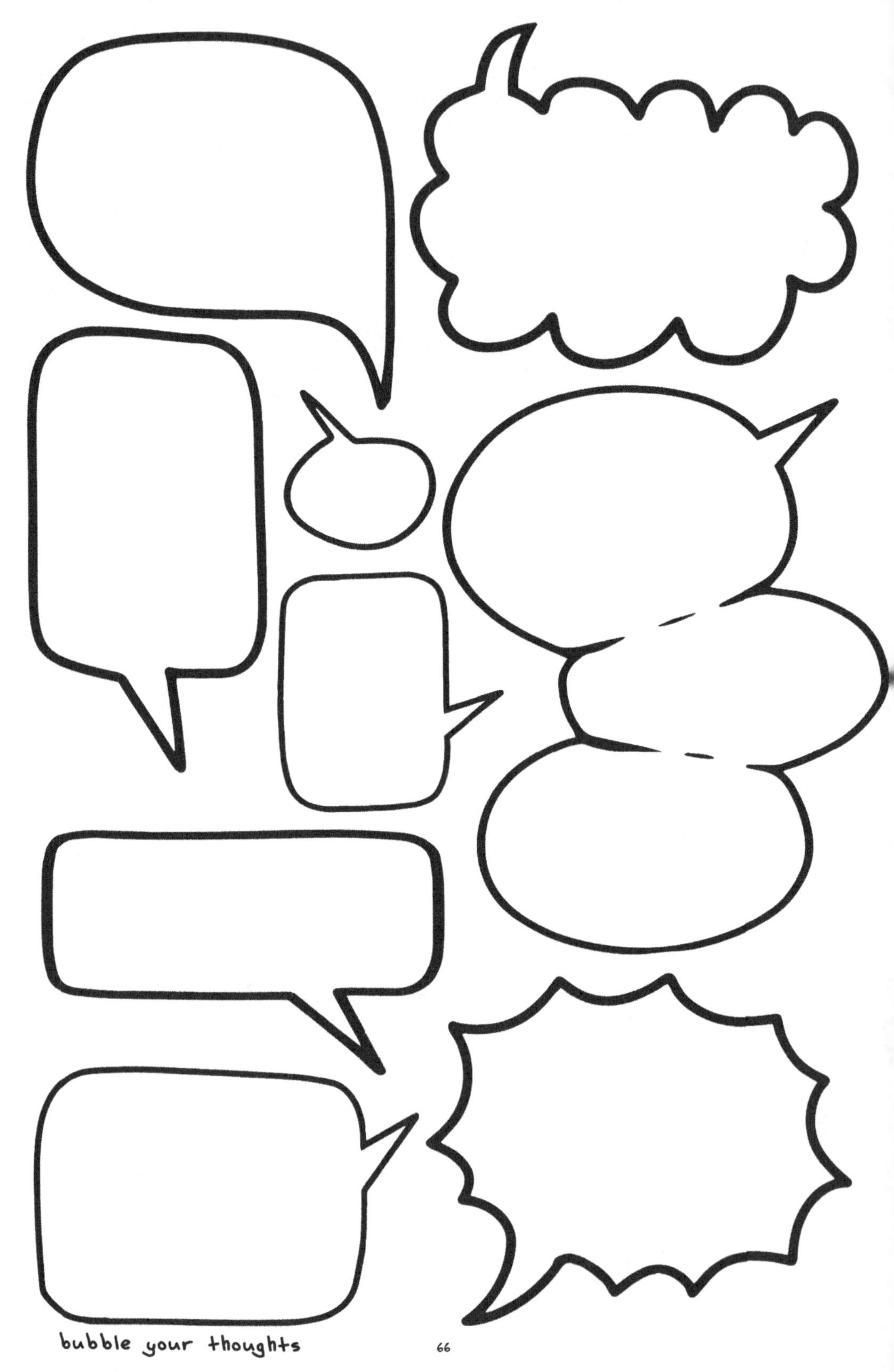

bubble your thoughts

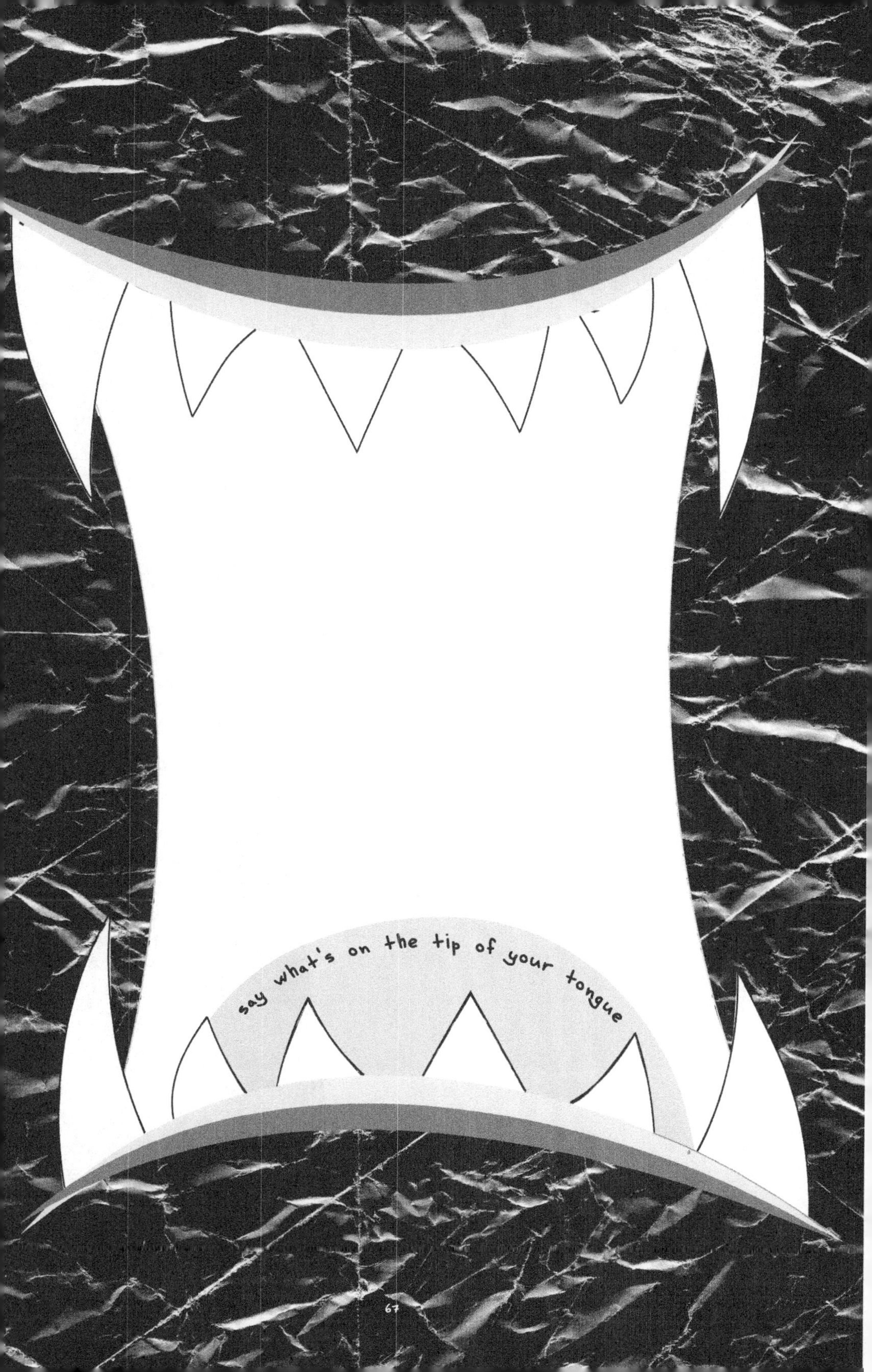

say what's on the tip of your tongue

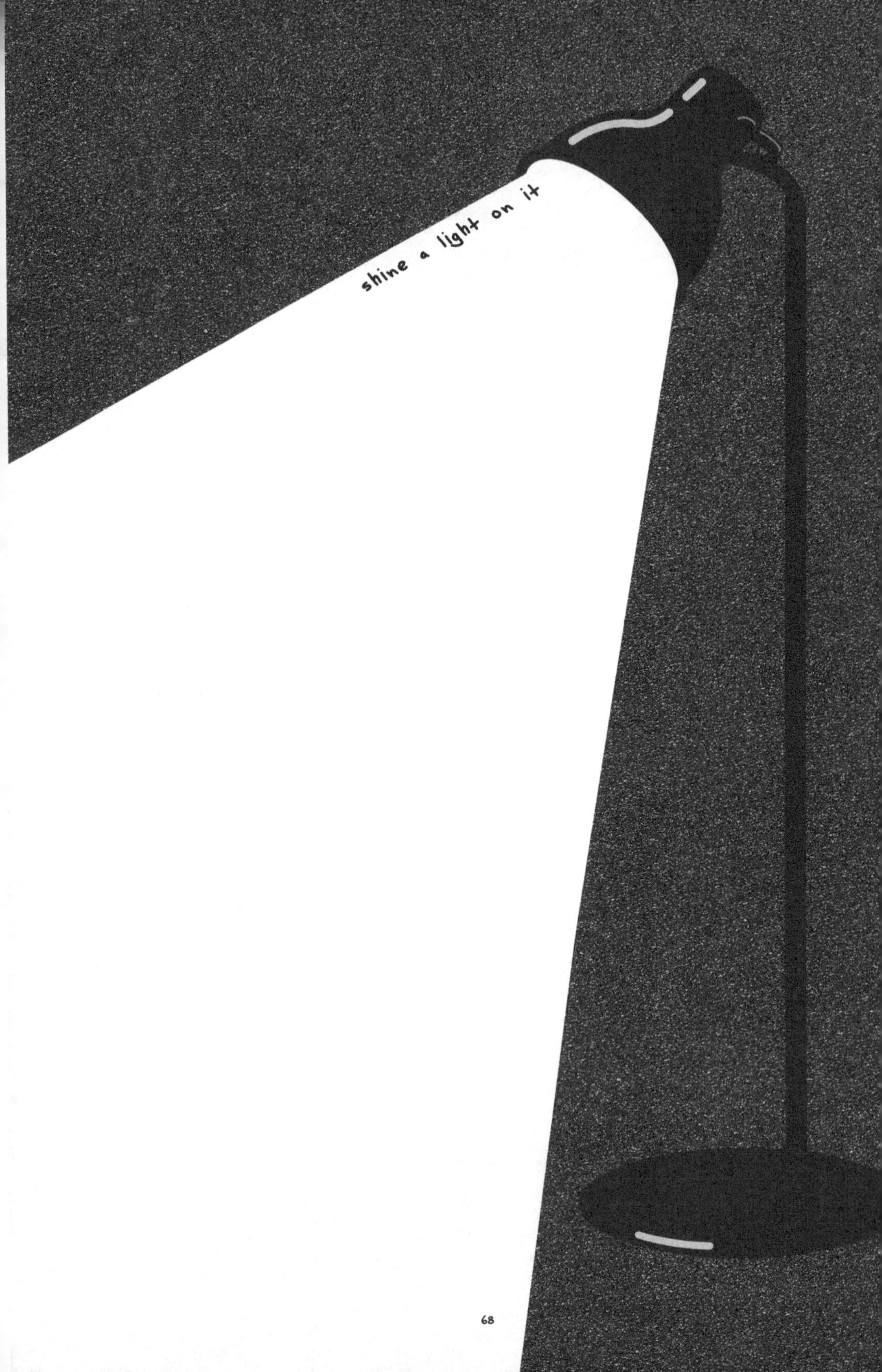
shine a light on it

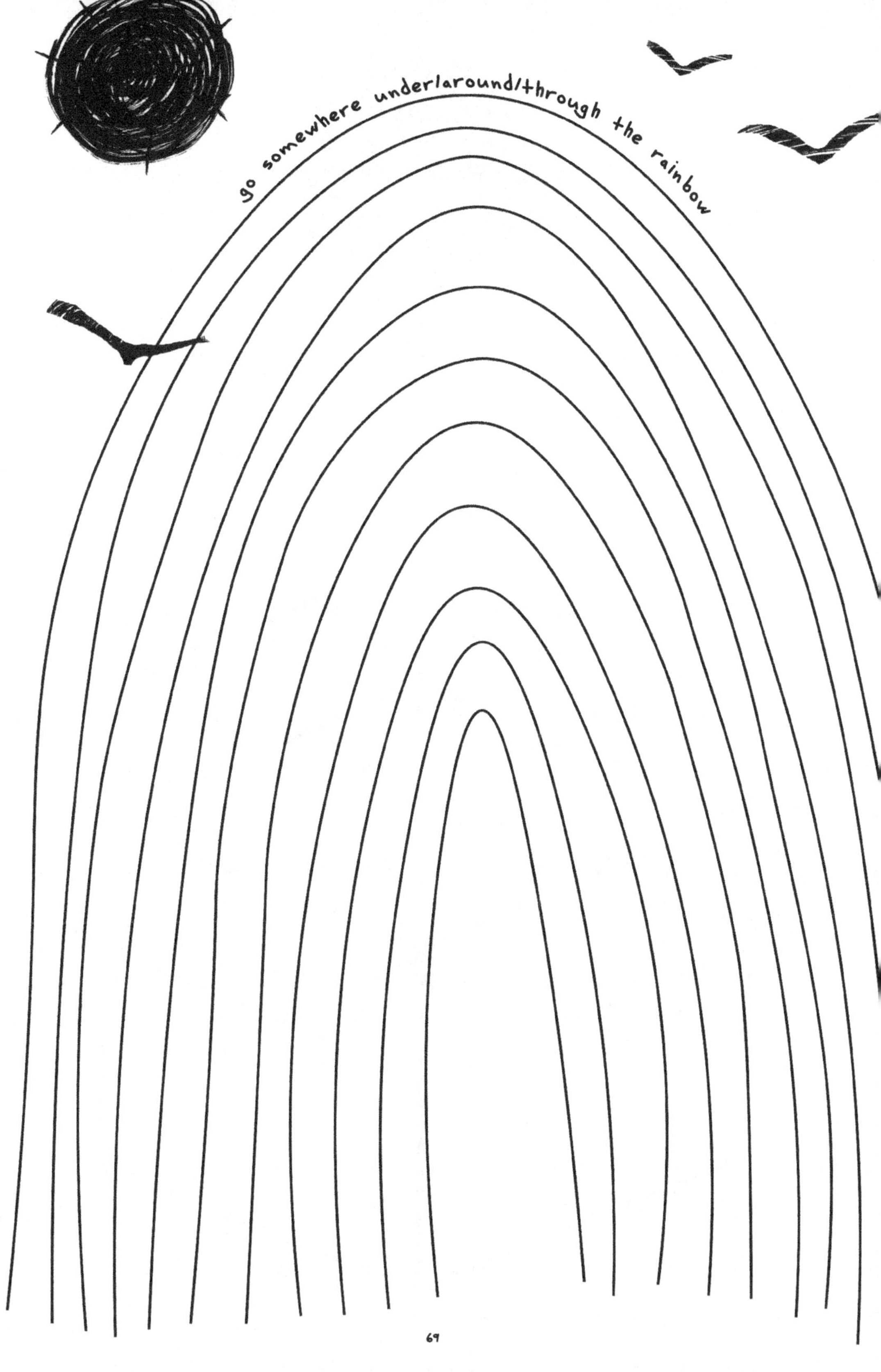

go somewhere under/around/through the rainbow

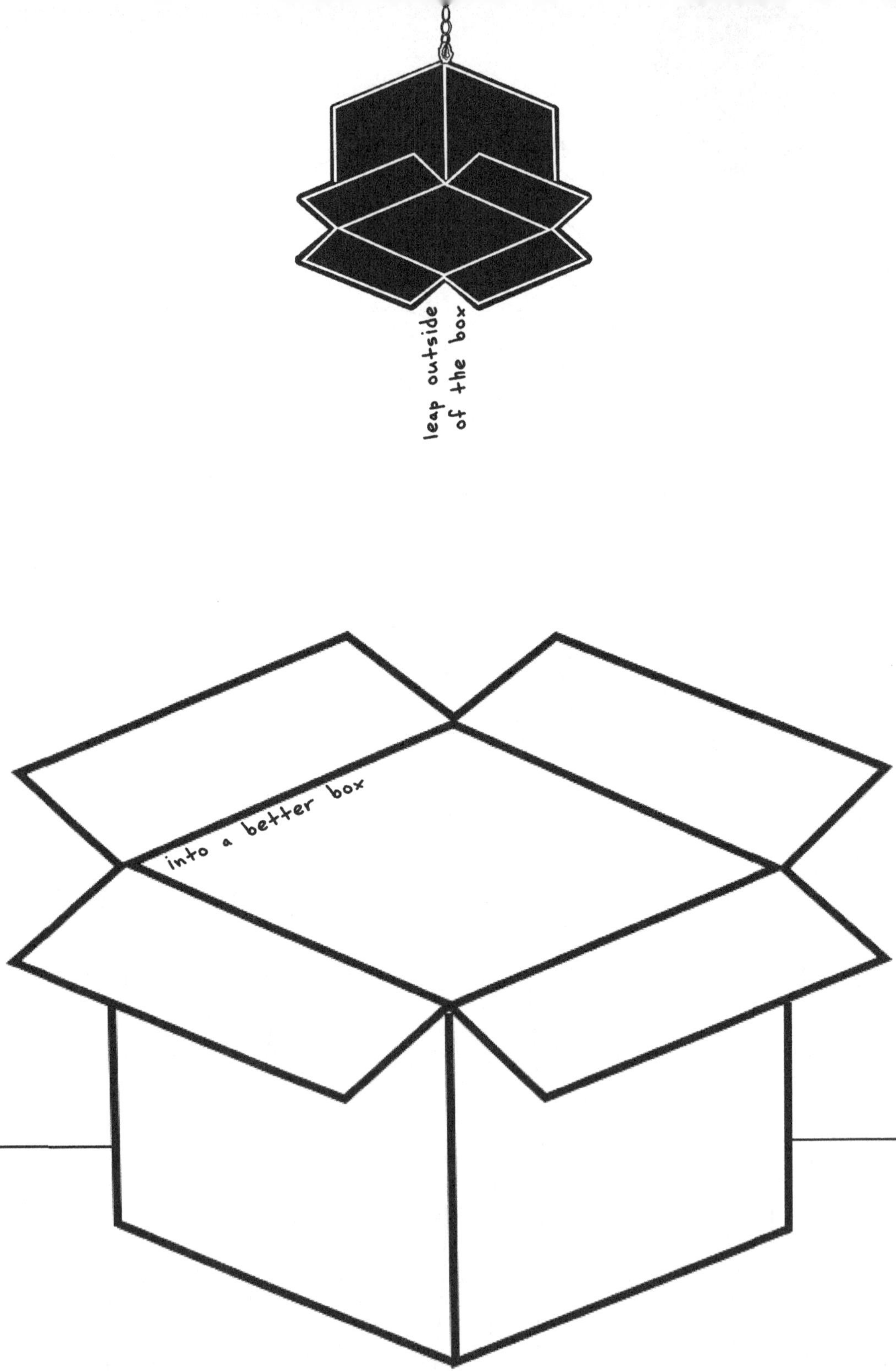

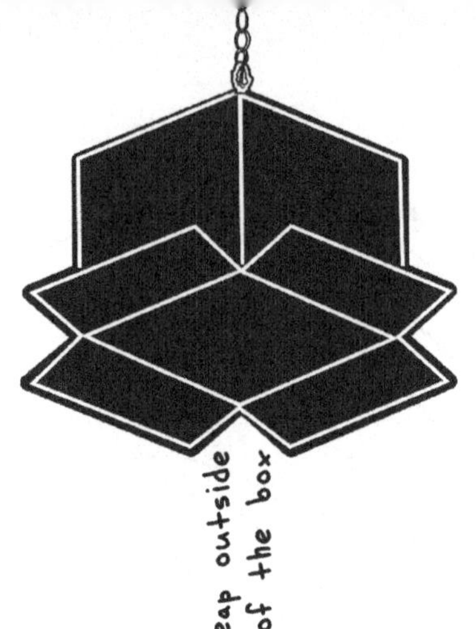

leap outside of the box

into a better box

write yourself out of a corner

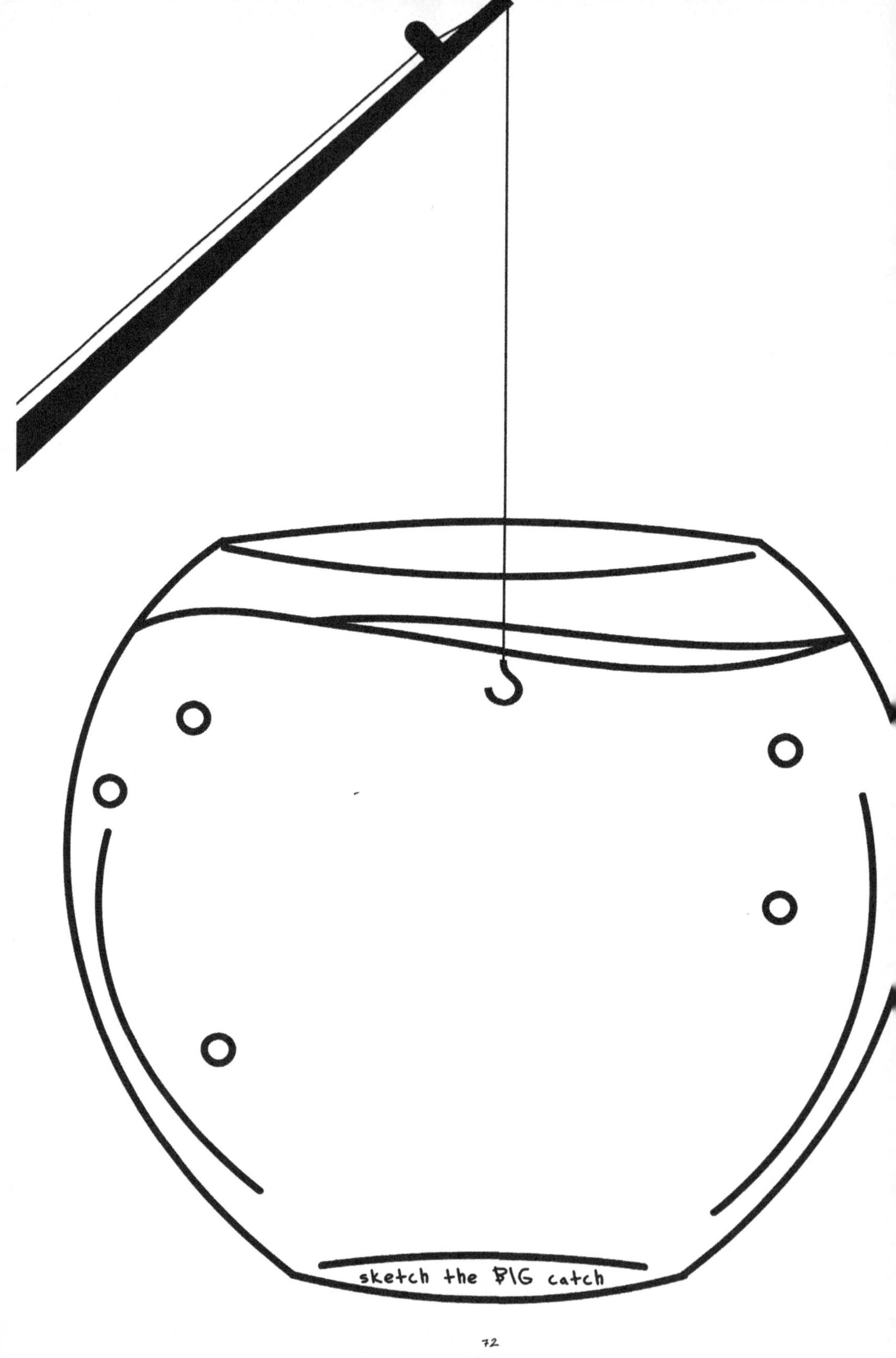
sketch the BIG catch

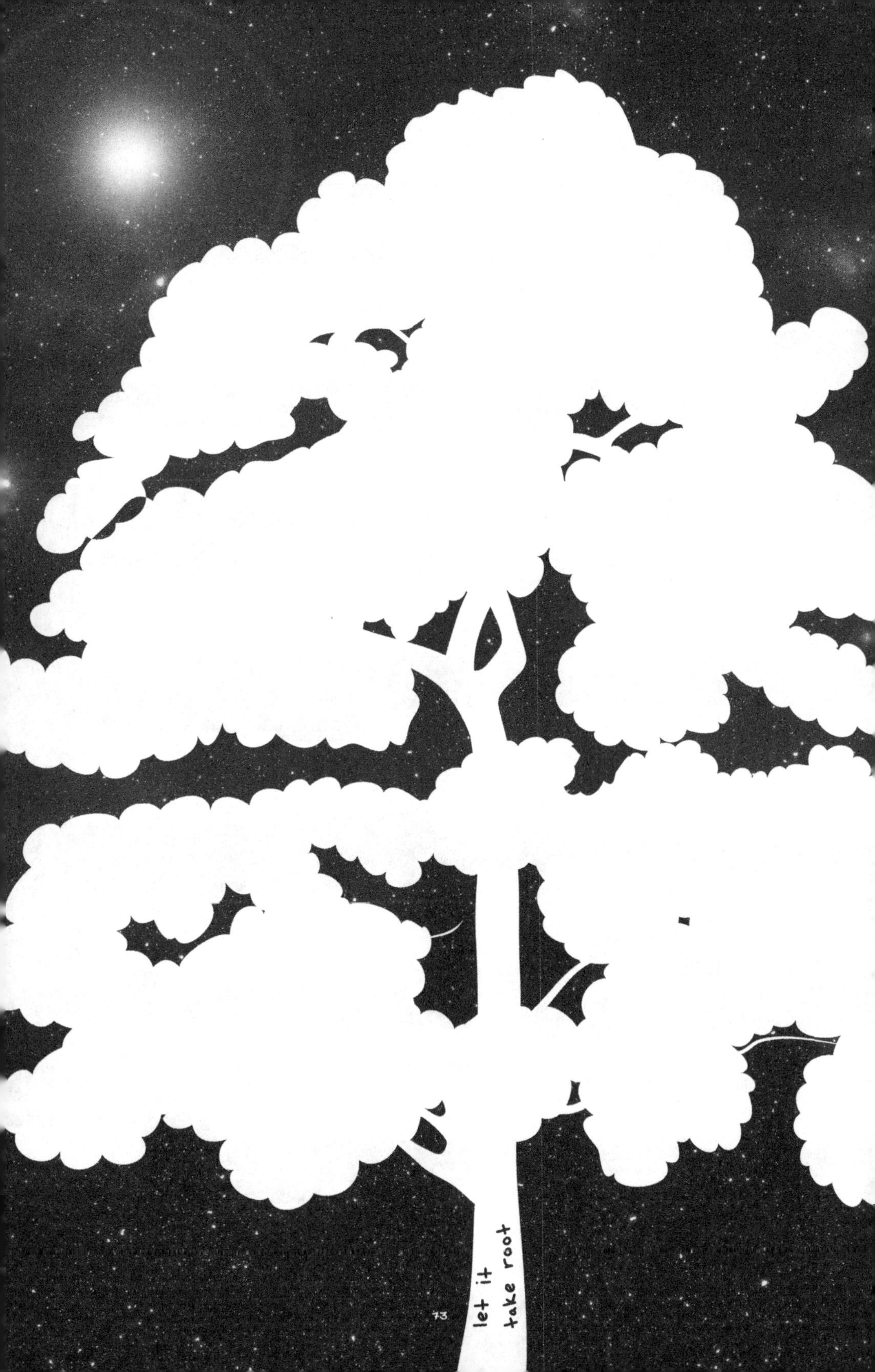
let it take root

un-redact it

turn it upside down
turn it upside down

negate the scribbles

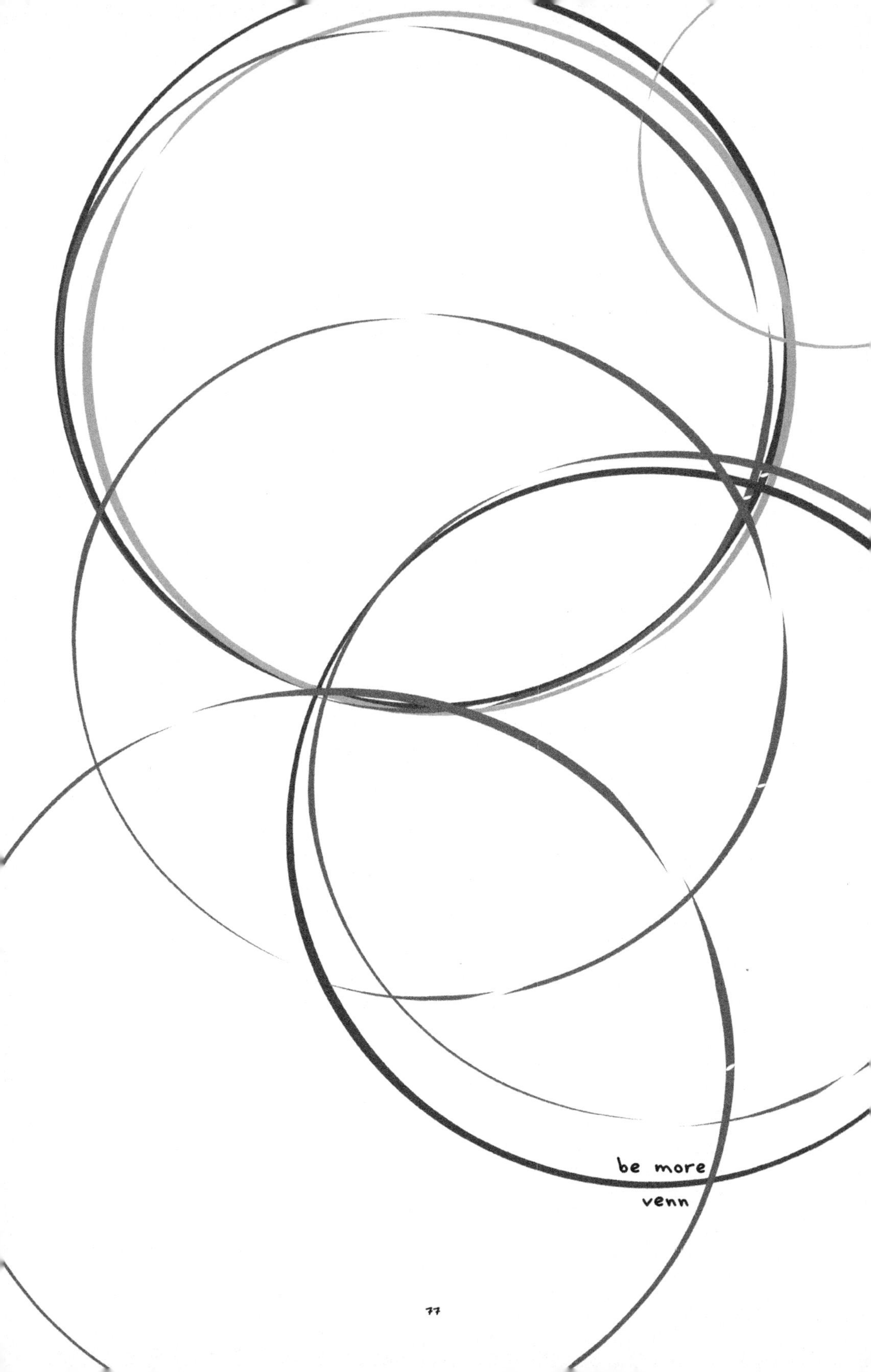
be more
venn

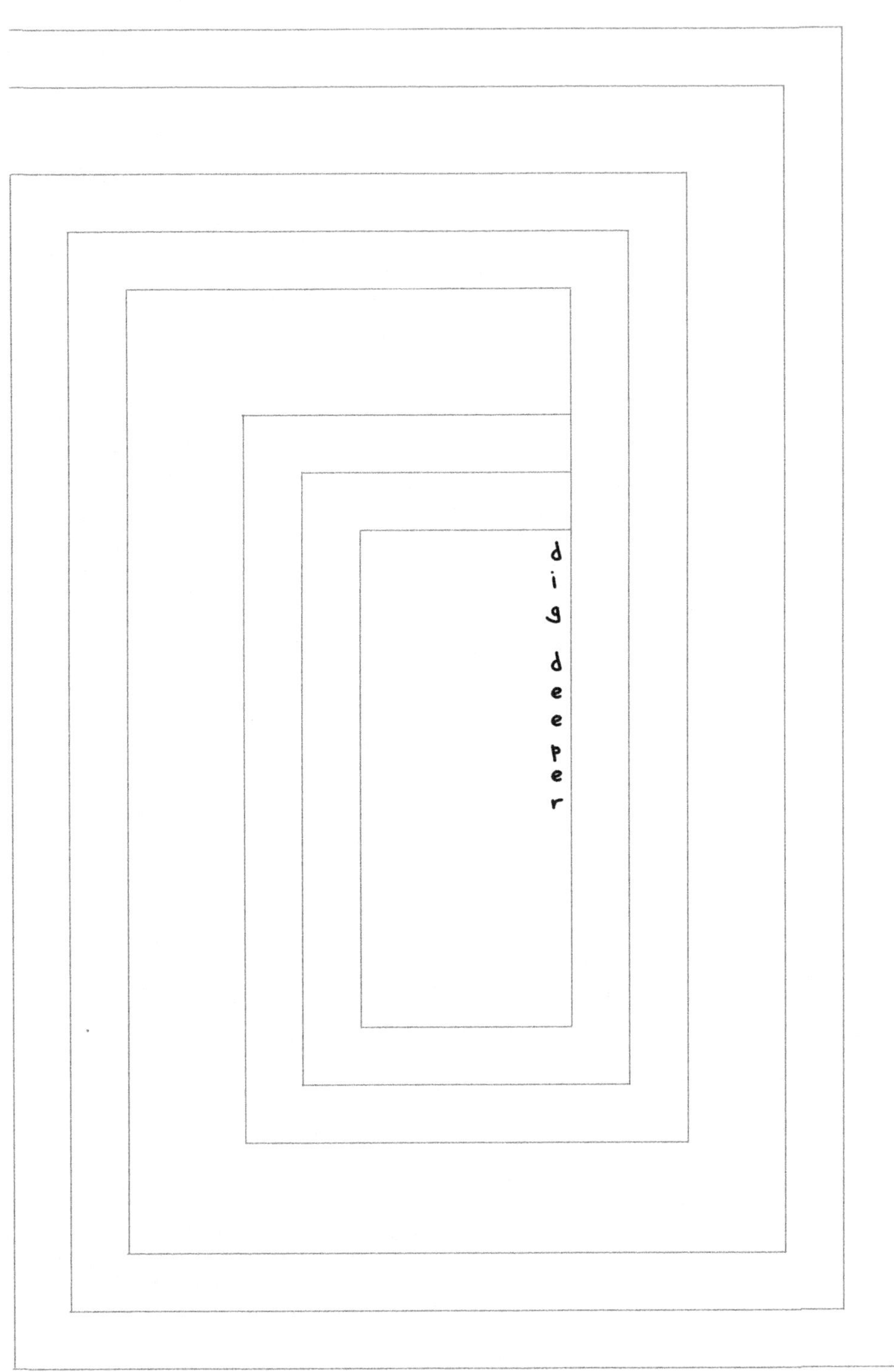

dig deeper

have a proper   brainstorm

vandalize it

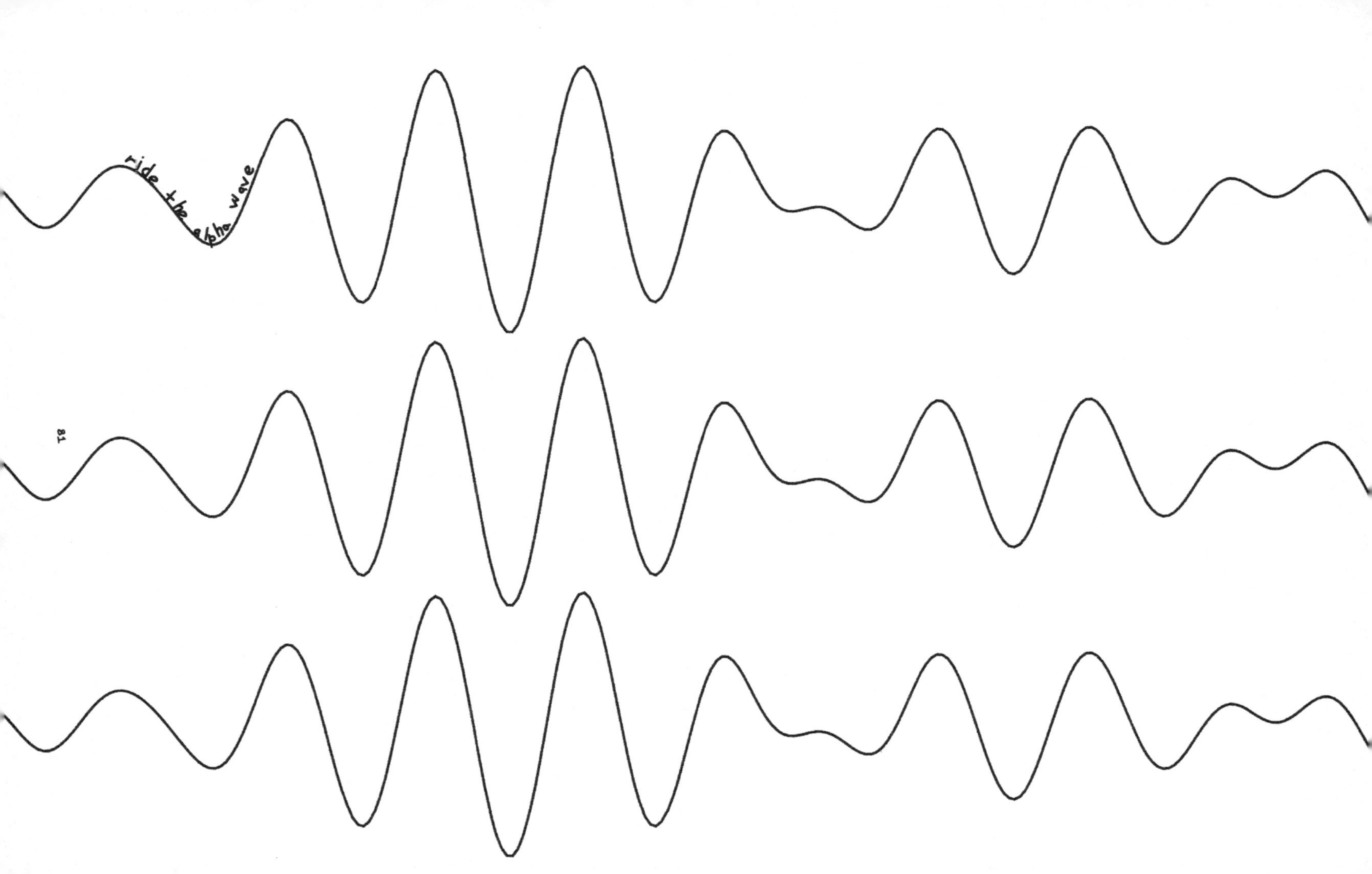
ride the alpha wave

set
it on
fire

AY.BLURT.SPILLIT.TELL.BEG.SCREAM.UTTER.PROCLAIM.EXPRESS.SPEAK.SHOUT.WHISPER.SPEW.AIRIT.YELL.CRYOUT.EXPLAIN.HOLLER.ECHO.BLARE.VOCALIZE.SPITITOUT.

STATE.PLEAD.BLABBER.MOUTH.COMMENT.SPOUT.REWORD.VENT.VOICE.DISCUSS.ARTICULATE.MUMBLE.SPIN.COMMENT.BLABBER.SAY.BLURT.REWORD.SPILLIT.ARTICULATE.TELL.

ANNOUNCE.BEG.SNARL.SCREAM.ELABORATE.UTTER.PROCLAIM.VENT.EXPRESS.SPEAK.SPOUT.STATE.SHOUT.WHISPER.SPEW.PLEAD.AIR.YELL.CRYOUT.EXPLAIN.DECLARE.HOLLER.

DISCUSS.ECHO.BLARE.VOCALIZE.SPITITOUT.MOUTH.VOICE.ADMIT.SAY.BLURT.SPILLIT.TELL.BEG.SCREAM.UTTER.PROCLAIM.EXPRESS.SPEAK.SHOUT.WHISPER.SPEW.AIRIT.

ELL.CRYOUT.EXPLAIN.HOLLER.ECHO.BLARE.VOCALIZE.SPITITOUT.STATE.PLEAD.BLABBER.MOUTH.COMMENT.SPOUT.REWORD.VENT.VOICE.DISCUSS.ARTICULATE.MUMBLE.SPIN.

COMMENT.BLABBER.SAY.BLURT.REWORD.SPILLIT.ARTICULATE.TELL.ANNOUNCE.BEG.ADMIT.SNARL.SCREAM.ELABORATE.UTTER.PROCLAIM.VENT.EXPRESS.SPEAK.SPOUT.STATE.

SHOUT.WHISPER.SPEW.PLEAD.AIR.YELL.CRYOUT.EXPLAIN.DECLARE.HOLLER.DISCUSS.ECHO.BLARE.VOCALIZE.SPITITOUT.MOUTH.VOICE.SAY.BLURT.SPILLIT.TELL.BEG.SCREAM.

UTTER.PROCLAIM.EXPRESS.SPEAK.SHOUT.WHISPER.SPEW.AIRIT.YELL.CRYOUT.EXPLAIN.HOLLER.ECHO.BLARE.VOCALIZE.SPITITOUT.STATE.PLEAD.BLABBER.MOUTH.COMMENT.SPOUT.

REWORD.VENT.VOICE.DISCUSS.ARTICULATE.ADMIT.MUMBLE.SPIN.COMMENT.BLABBER.SAY.BLURT.REWORD.SPILLIT.ARTICULATE.TELL.ANNOUNCE.BEG.SNARL.SCREAM.ELABORATE.

UTTER.PROCLAIM.VENT.EXPRESS.SPEAK.SPOUT.STATE.SHOUT.WHISPER.SPEW.PLEAD.AIR.YELL.CRYOUT.EXPLAIN.DECLARE.HOLLER.DISCUSS.ECHO.BLARE.VOCALIZE.SPITITOUT.

MOUTH.VOICE.SAY.BLURT.SPILLIT.TELL.BEG.SCREAM.UTTER.PROCLAIM.EXPRESS.SPEAK.SHOUT.WHISPER.SPEW.AIRIT.YELL.CRYOUT.EXPLAIN.HOLLER.ECHO.BLARE.

VOCALIZE.SPITITOUT.STATE.PLEAD.BLABBER.MOUTH.COMMENT.SPOUT.REWORD.VENT.VOICE.DISCUSS.ARTICULATE.MUMBLE.SPIN.COMMENT.BLABBER.SAY.BLURT.REWORD.SPILLIT.

ARTICULATE.TELL.ANNOUNCE.BEG.SNARL.SCREAM.ELABORATE.UTTER.PROCLAIM.VENT.EXPRESS.SPEAK.SPOUT.STATE.SHOUT.WHISPER.SPEW.PLEAD.AIR.YELL.CRYOUT.

EXPLAIN.DECLARE.HOLLER.DISCUSS.ECHO.BLARE.VOCALIZE.SPITITOUT.MOUTH.VOICE.SAY.BLURT.SPILLIT.SUGGEST.TELL.BEG.SCREAM.UTTER.PROCLAIM.EXPRESS.SPEAK.SHOUT.

WHISPER.SPEW.AIRIT.YELL.CRYOUT.EXPLAIN.HOLLER.ECHO.BLARE.VOCALIZE.SPITITOUT.STATE.PLEAD.BLABBER.MOUTH.COMMENT.SPOUT.REWORD.VENT.VOICE.DISCUSS.

ARTICULATE.MUMBLE.SPIN.COMMENT.BLABBER.SAY.BLURT.REWORD.SPILLIT.ARTICULATE.TELL.ANNOUNCE.BEG.SNARL.SCREAM.ELABORATE.UTTER.PROCLAIM.VENT.EXPRESS.SPEAK.

SPOUT.STATE.SHOUT.WHISPER.SPEW.PLEAD.AIR.YELL.CRYOUT.EXPLAIN.DECLARE.HOLLER.DISCUSS.ECHO.BLARE.VOCALIZE.SPITITOUT.MOUTH.VOICE.SAY.BLURT.SPILLIT.

TELL.BEG.SCREAM.UTTER.PROCLAIM.EXPRESS.SUGGEST.SPEAK.SHOUT.WHISPER.SPEW.AIRIT.YELL.CRYOUT.EXPLAIN.HOLLER.ECHO.BLARE.VOCALIZE.SPITITOUT.STATE.PLEAD.

BLABBER.ADMIT.MOUTH.COMMENT.SPOUT.REWORD.VENT.VOICE.DISCUSS.ARTICULATE.MUMBLE.SPIN.COMMENT.BLABBER.SAY.BLURT.REWORD.SPILLIT.ARTICULATE.TELL.

ANNOUNCE.BEG.SNARL.SCREAM.ELABORATE.UTTER.PROCLAIM.VENT.EXPRESS.SPEAK.SPOUT.STATE.SHOUT.WHISPER.SPEW.PLEAD.AIR.YELL.CRYOUT.EXPLAIN.SUGGEST.DECLARE.

HOLLER.DISCUSS.ECHO.BLARE.VOCALIZE.SPITITOUT.MOUTH.VOICE.SAY.BLURT.SPILLIT.TELL.BEG.SCREAM.UTTER.PROCLAIM.EXPRESS.SPEAK.SHOUT.WHISPER.SPEW.AIRIT.YELL.

CRYOUT.EXPLAIN.HOLLER.ECHO.ADMIT.BLARE.VOCALIZE.SPITITOUT.STATE.PLEAD.BLABBER.MOUTH.COMMENT.SPOUT.REWORD.VENT.VOICE.DISCUSS.ARTICULATE.MUMBLE.SPIN.

COMMENT.BLABBER.SAY.BLURT.REWORD.SPILLIT.ARTICULATE.TELL.ANNOUNCE.BEG.SNARL.SCREAM.ELABORATE.UTTER.PROCLAIM.VENT.EXPRESS.SPEAK.SPOUT.STATE.SHOUT.

WHISPER.ADMIT.SPEW.PLEAD.AIR.YELL.CRYOUT.EXPLAIN.DECLARE.HOLLER.DISCUSS.ECHO.BLARE.VOCALIZE.SPITITOUT.MOUTH.VOICE.SAY.BLURT.SPILLIT.TELL.BEG.SCREAM.

UTTER.PROCLAIM.EXPRESS.SPEAK.SHOUT.WHISPER.SPEW.AIRIT.YELL.CRYOUT.EXPLAIN.HOLLER.ECHO.BLARE.VOCALIZE.SPITITOUT.STATE.PLEAD.BLABBER.MOUTH.COMMENT.

think in between the lines

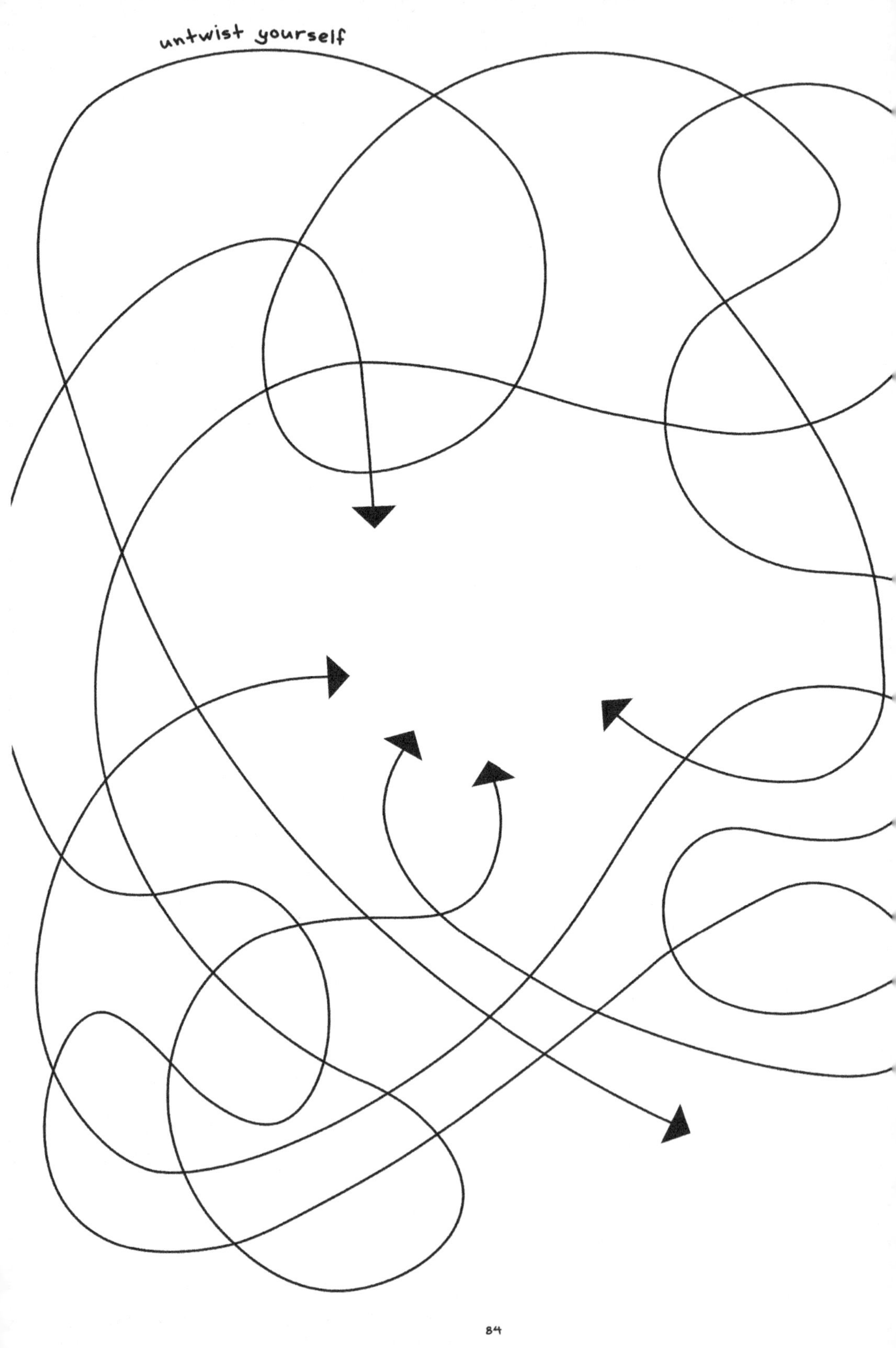
untwist yourself

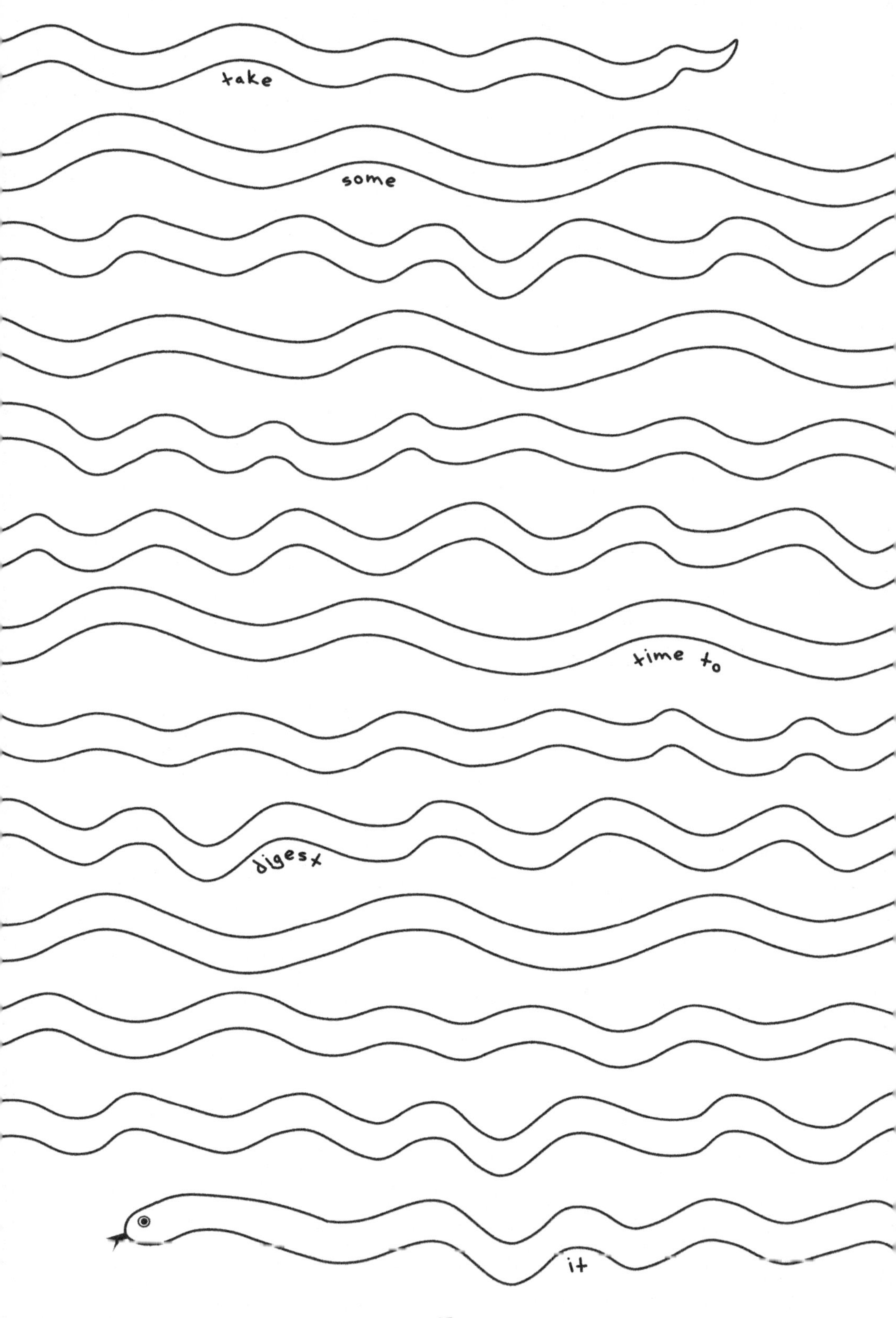

take
some
time to
digest
some
it

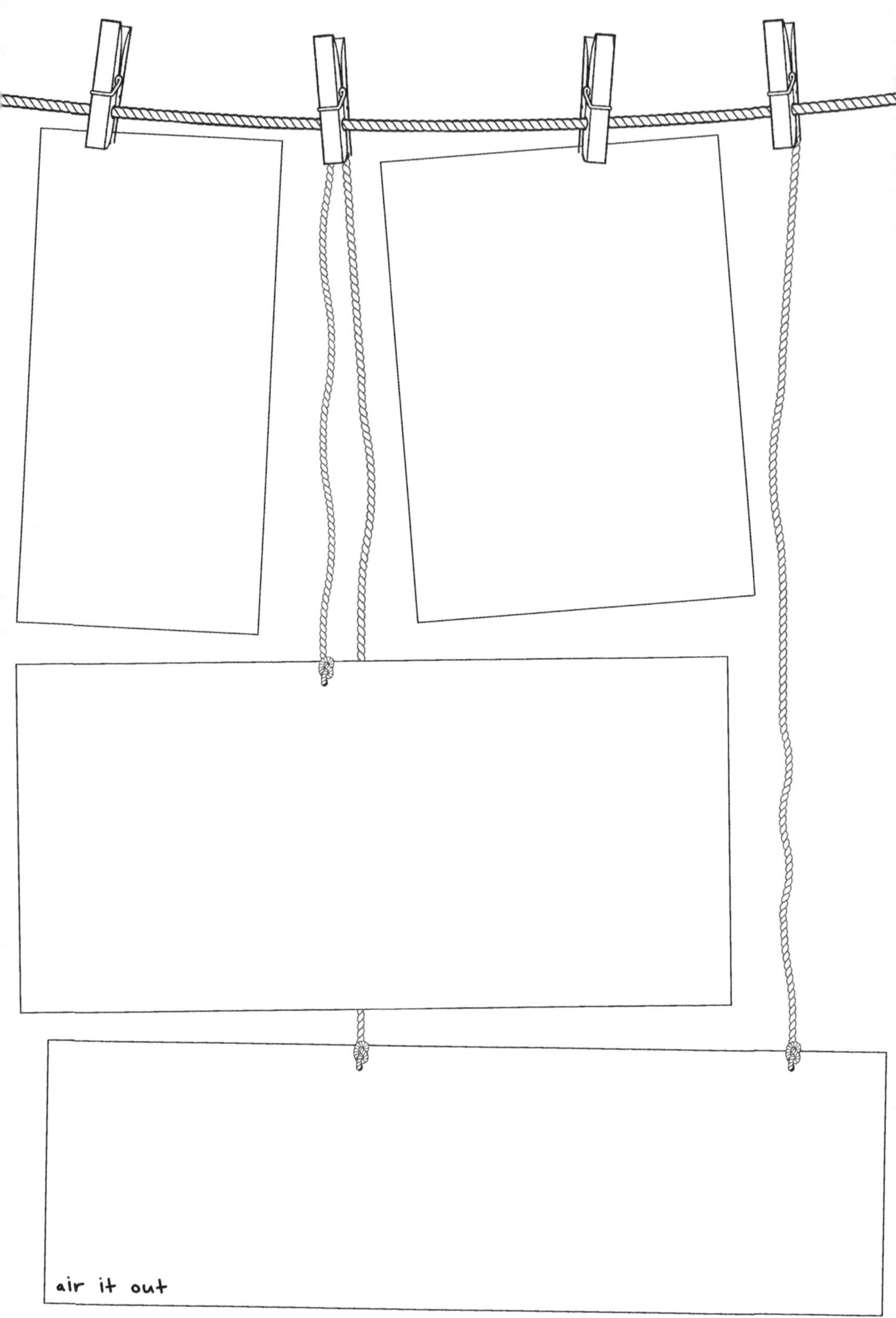
air it out
air it out

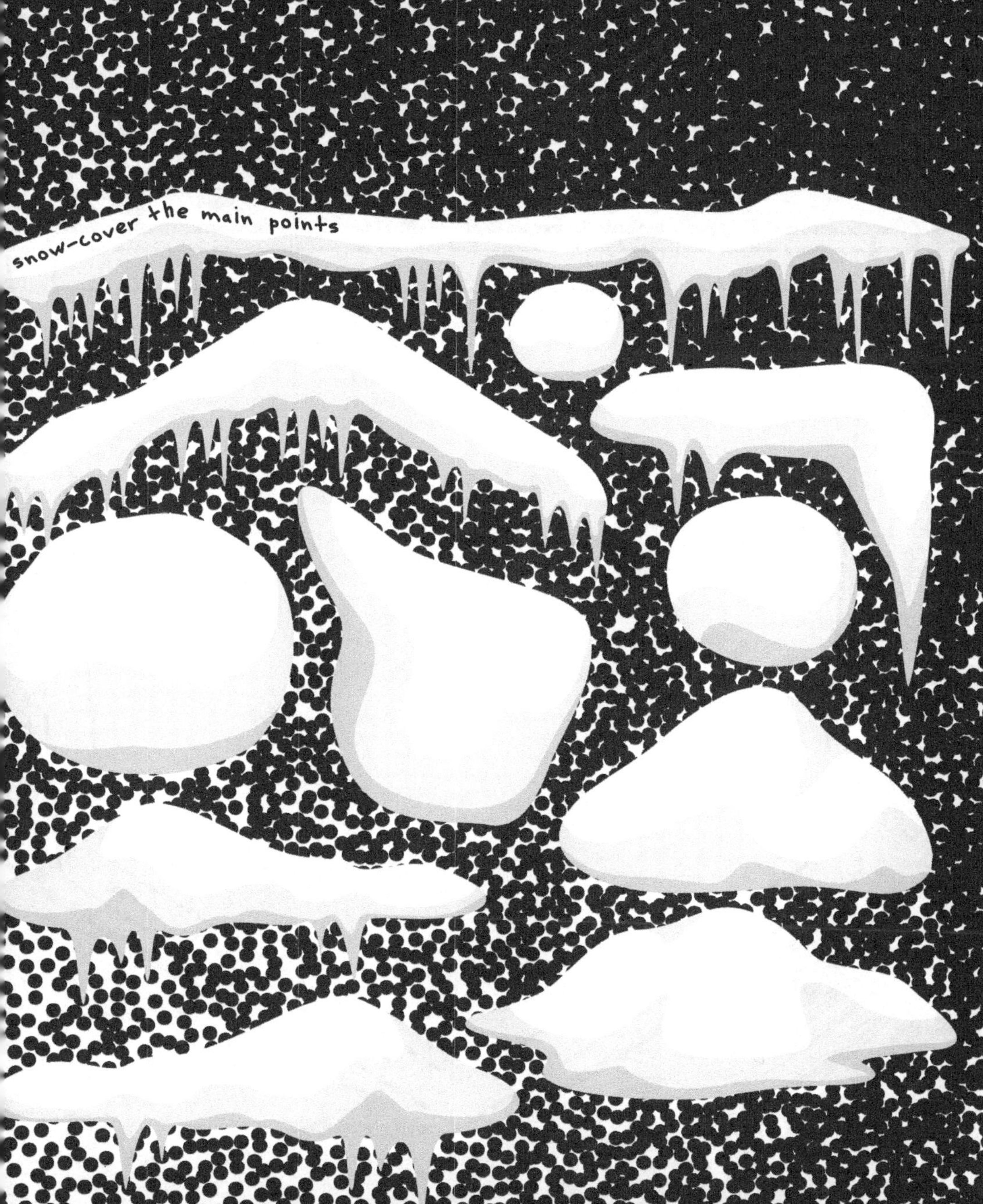

snow-cover the main points

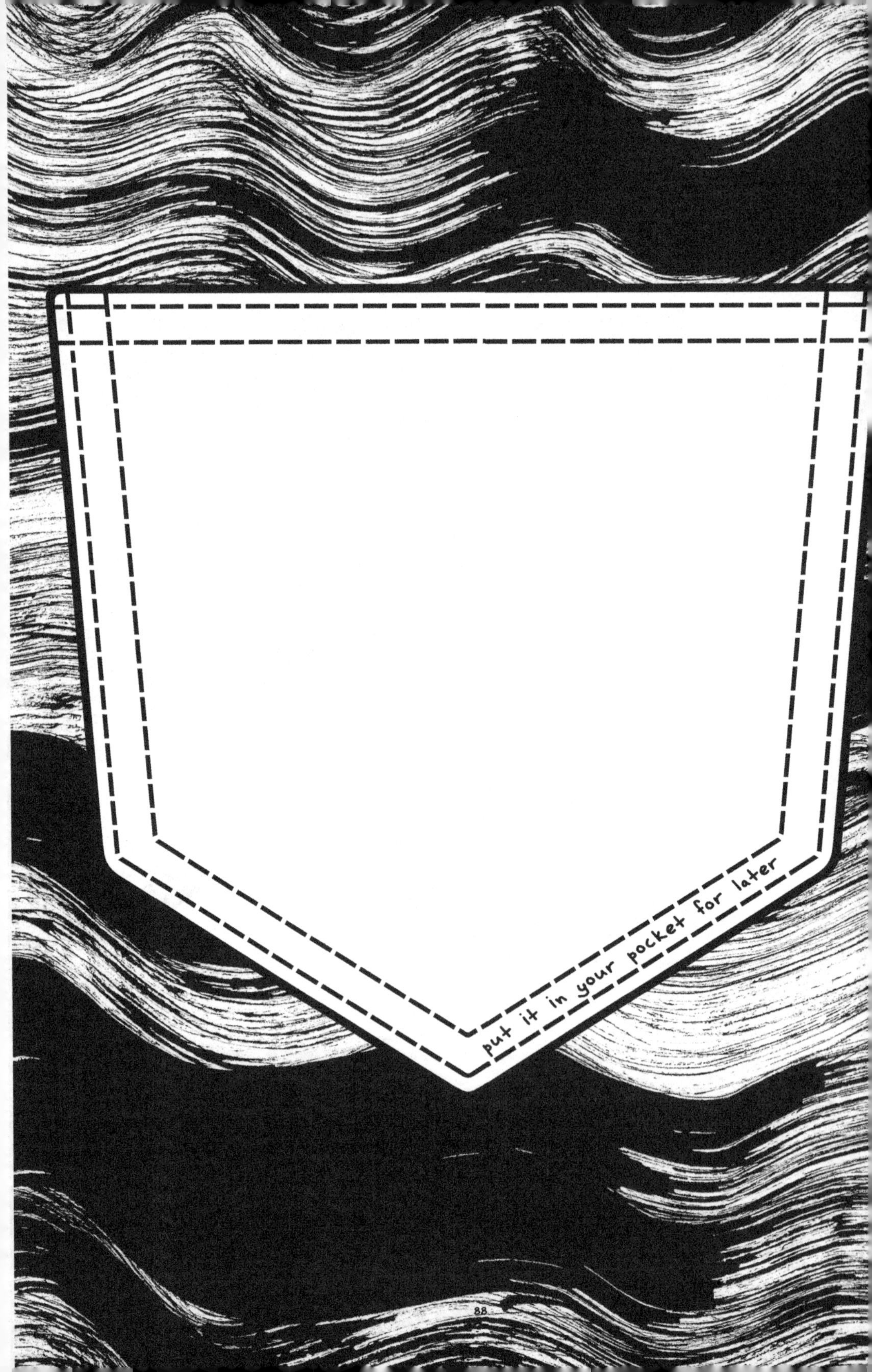
put it in your pocket for later

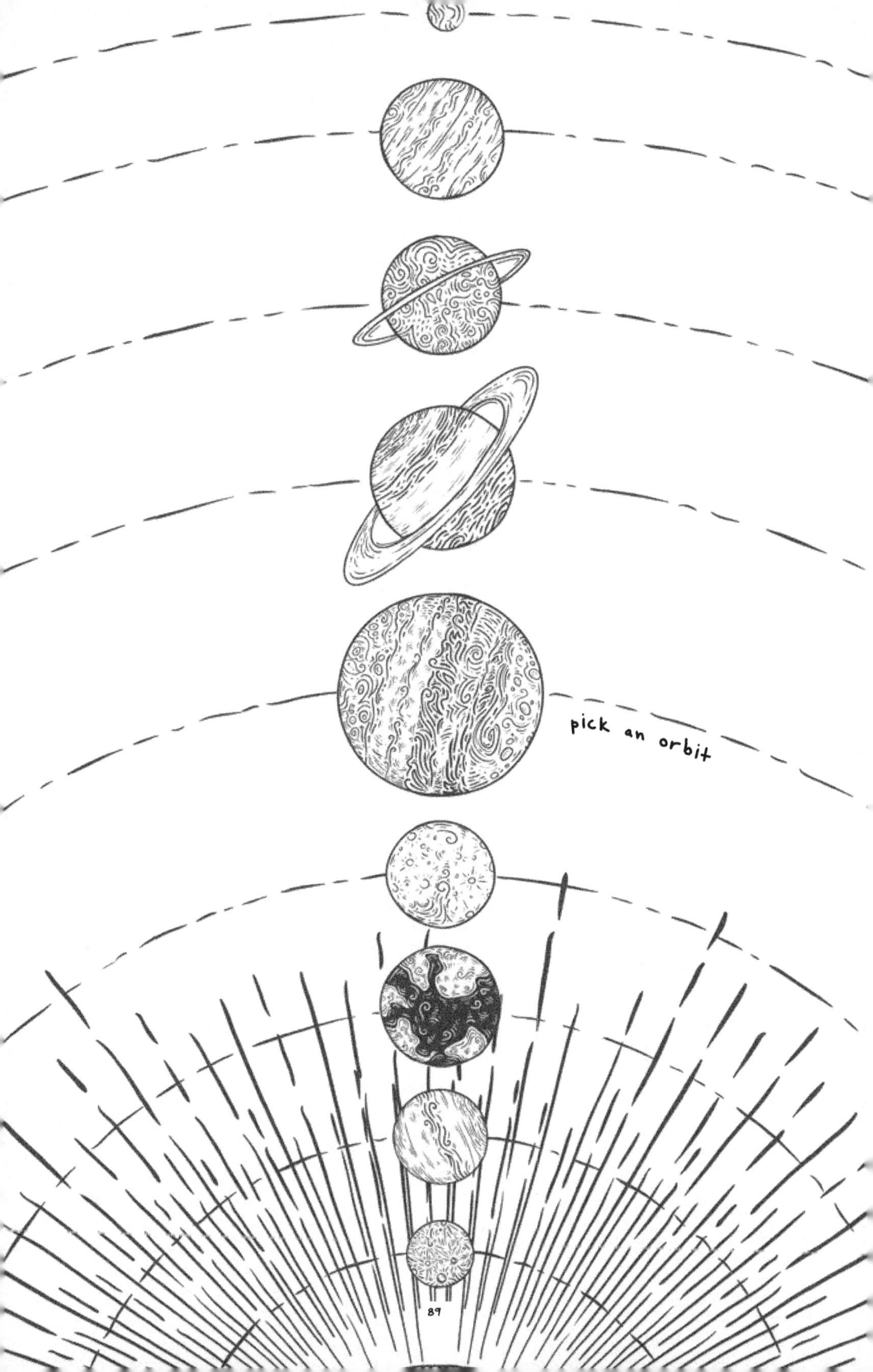

pick an orbit
89

float an idea

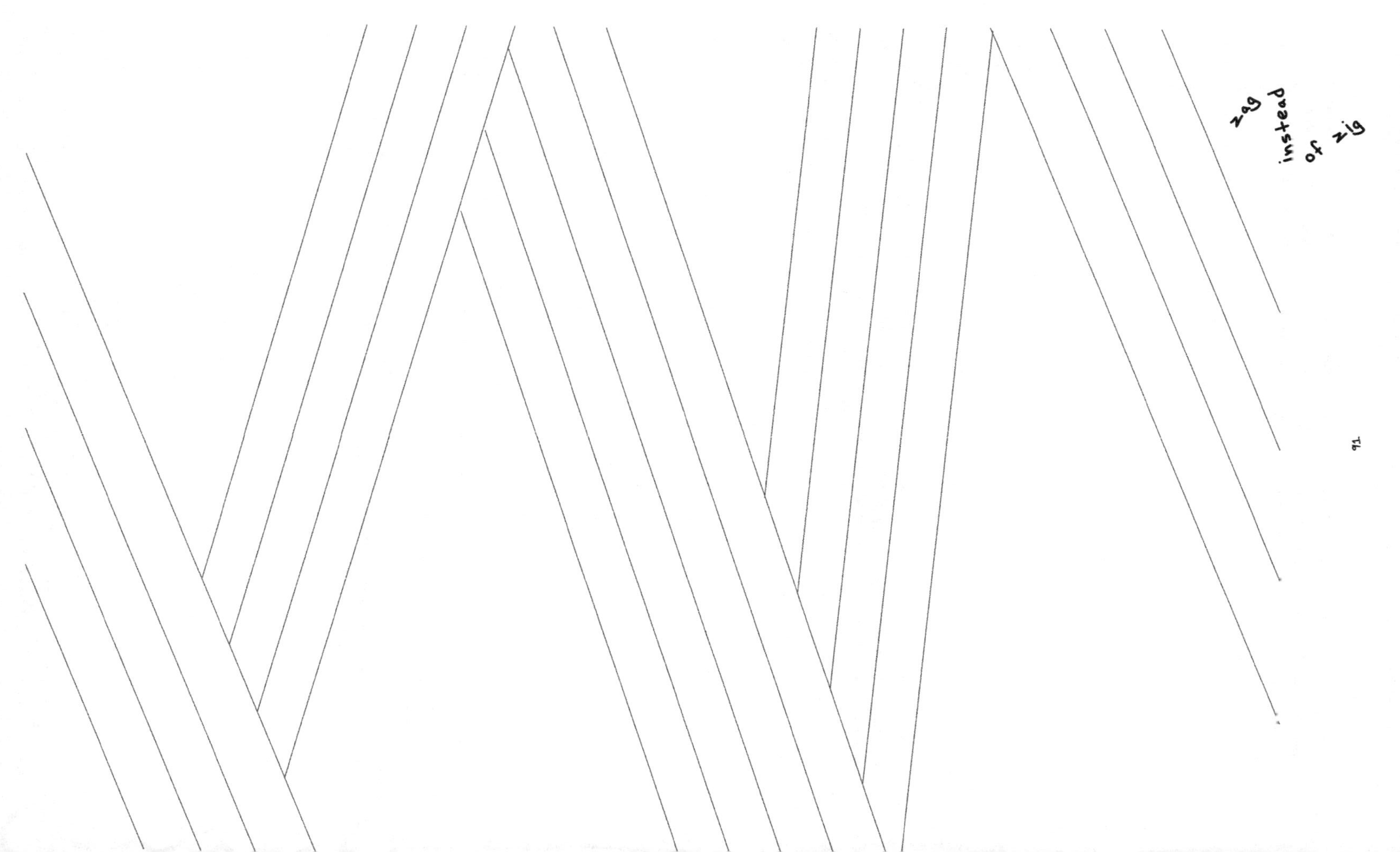

zag
instead
of zig

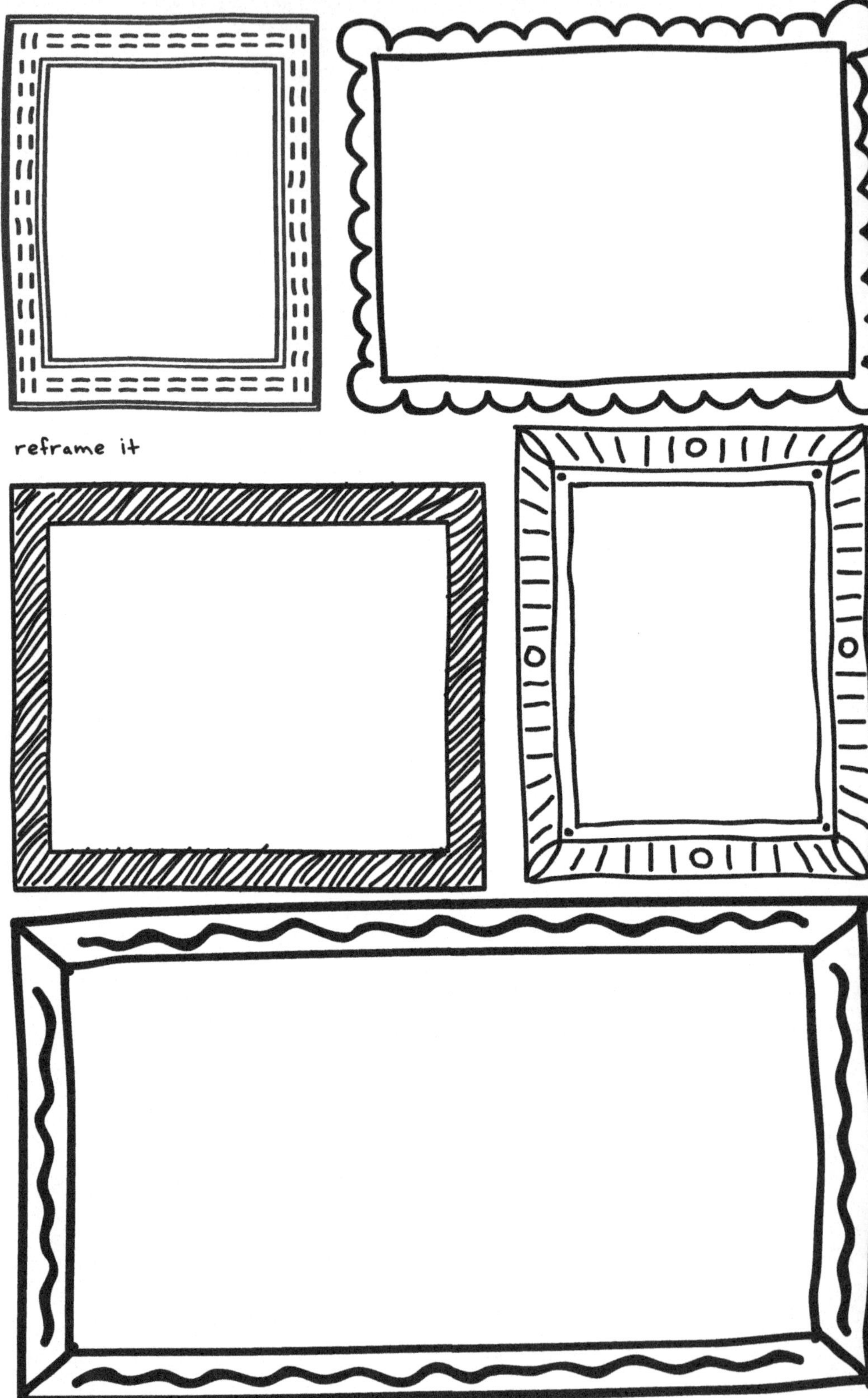

reframe it

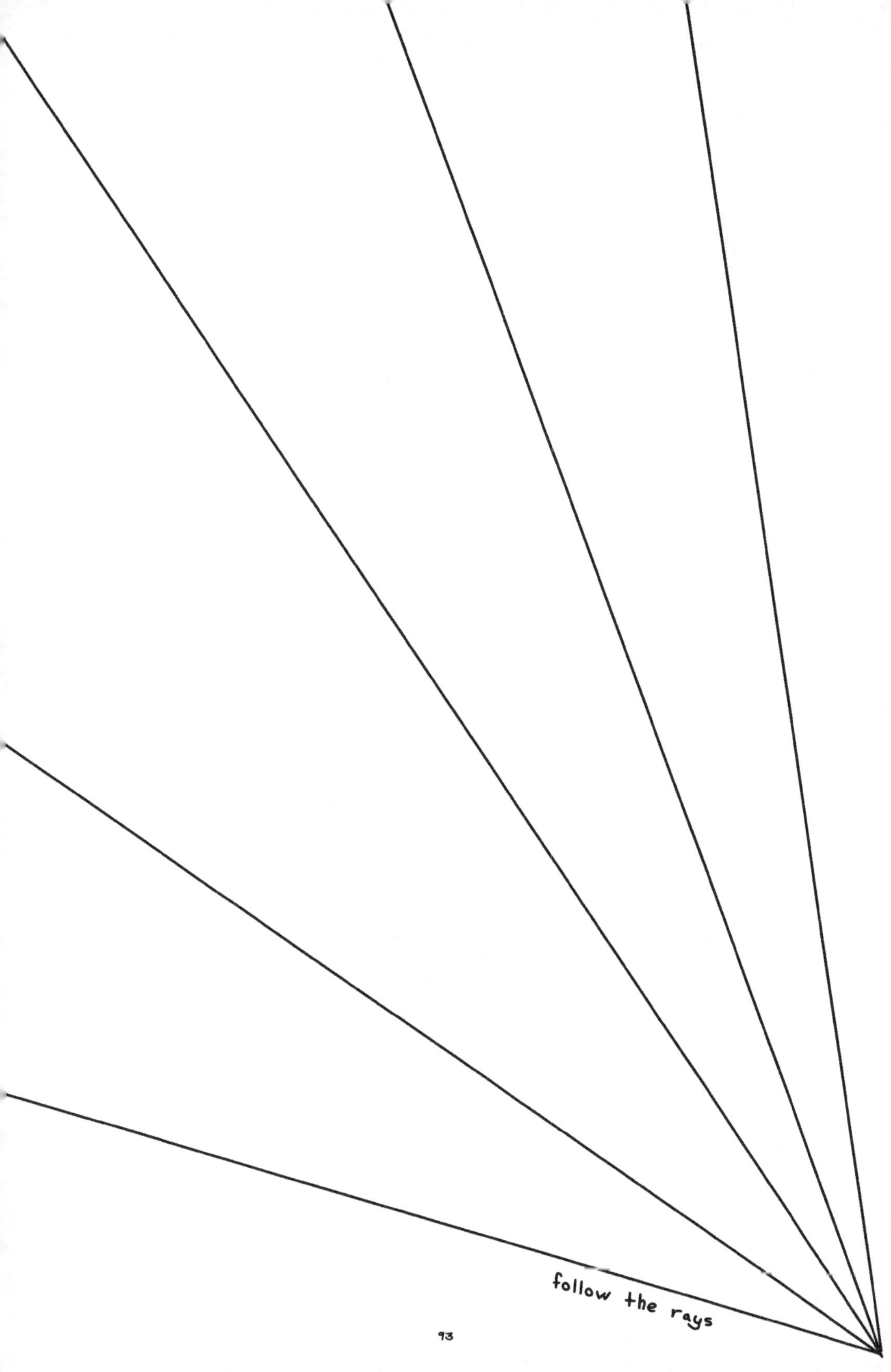
follow the rays

tilt
your
brain

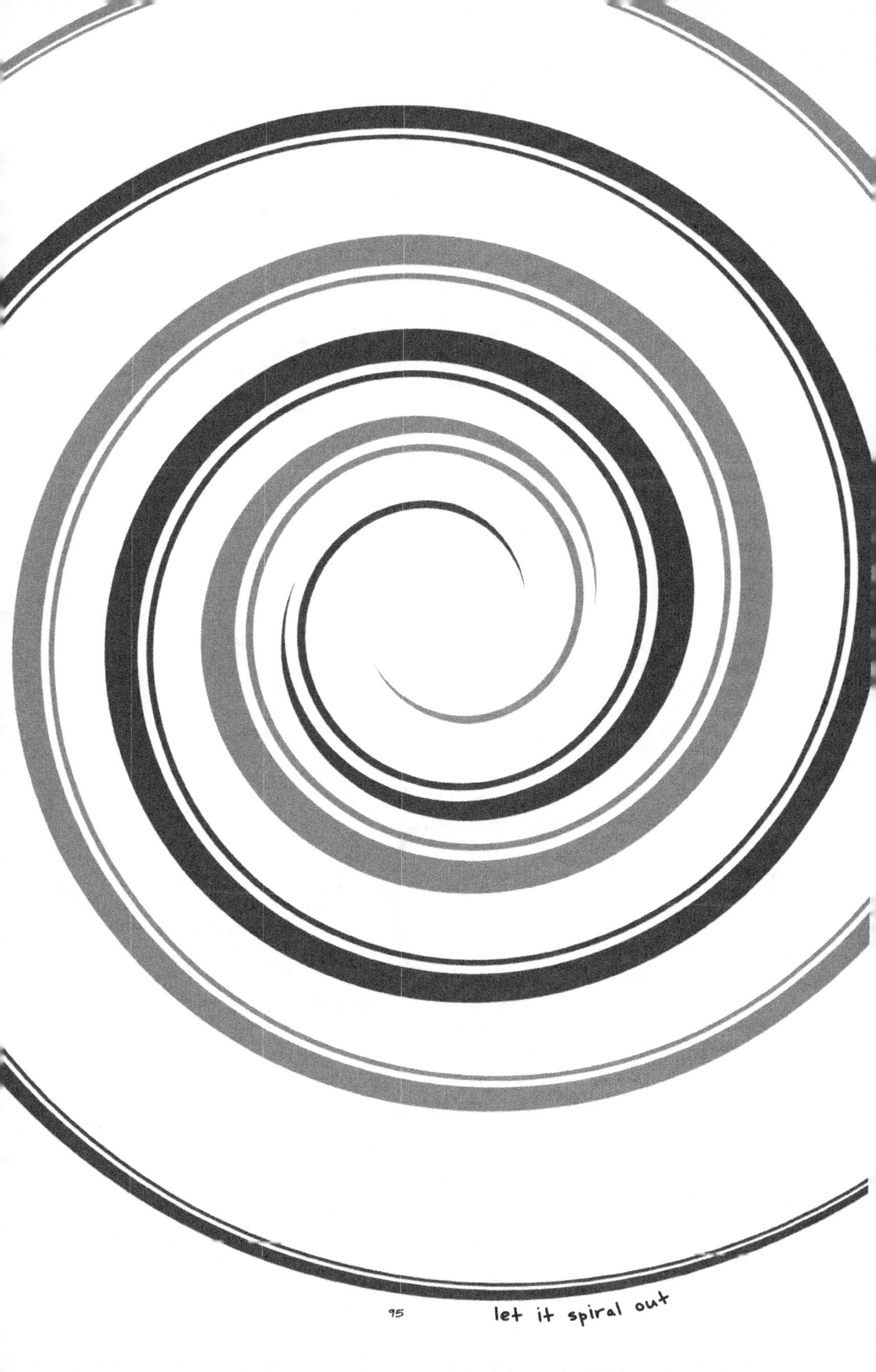

let it spiral out

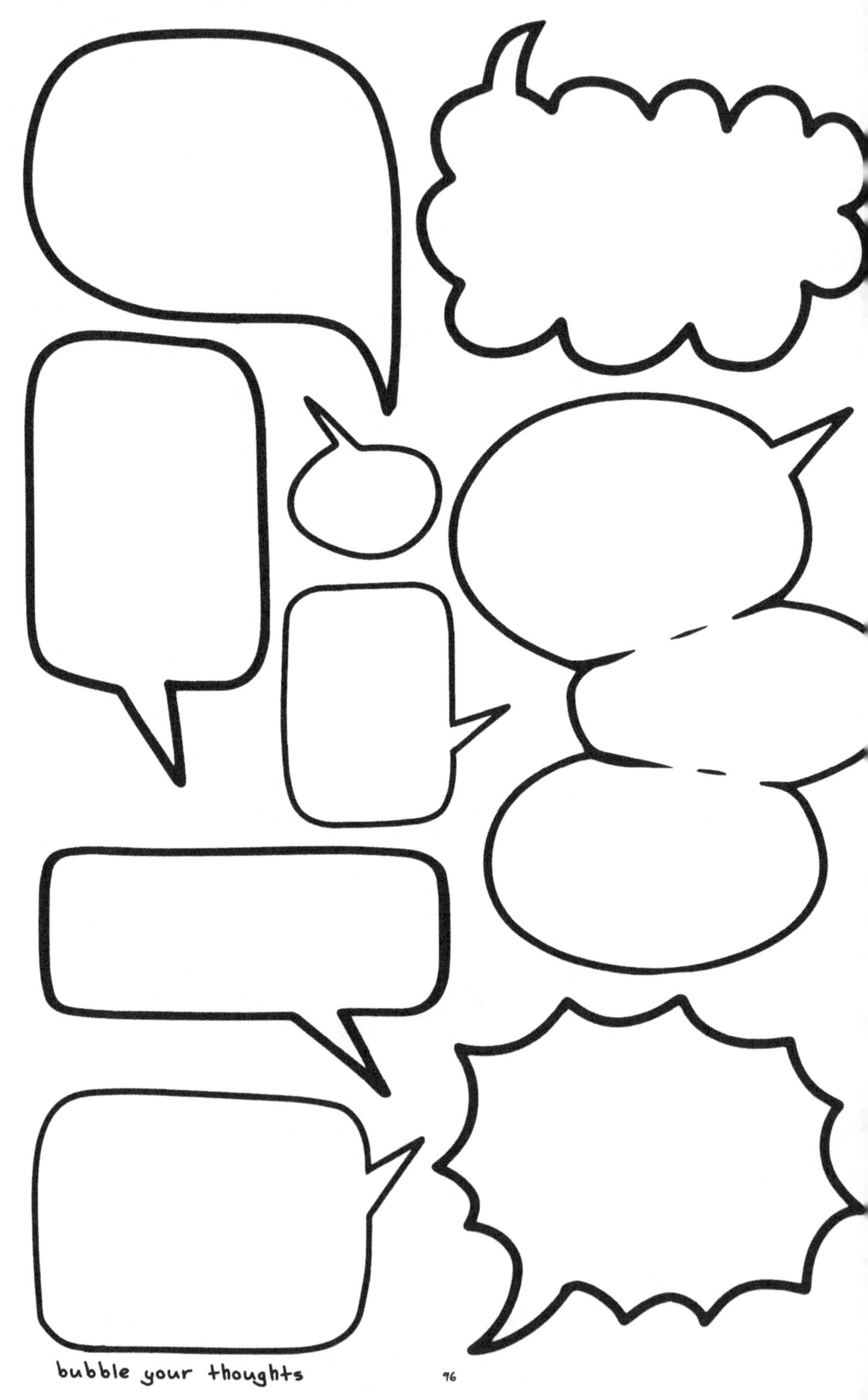
bubble your thoughts

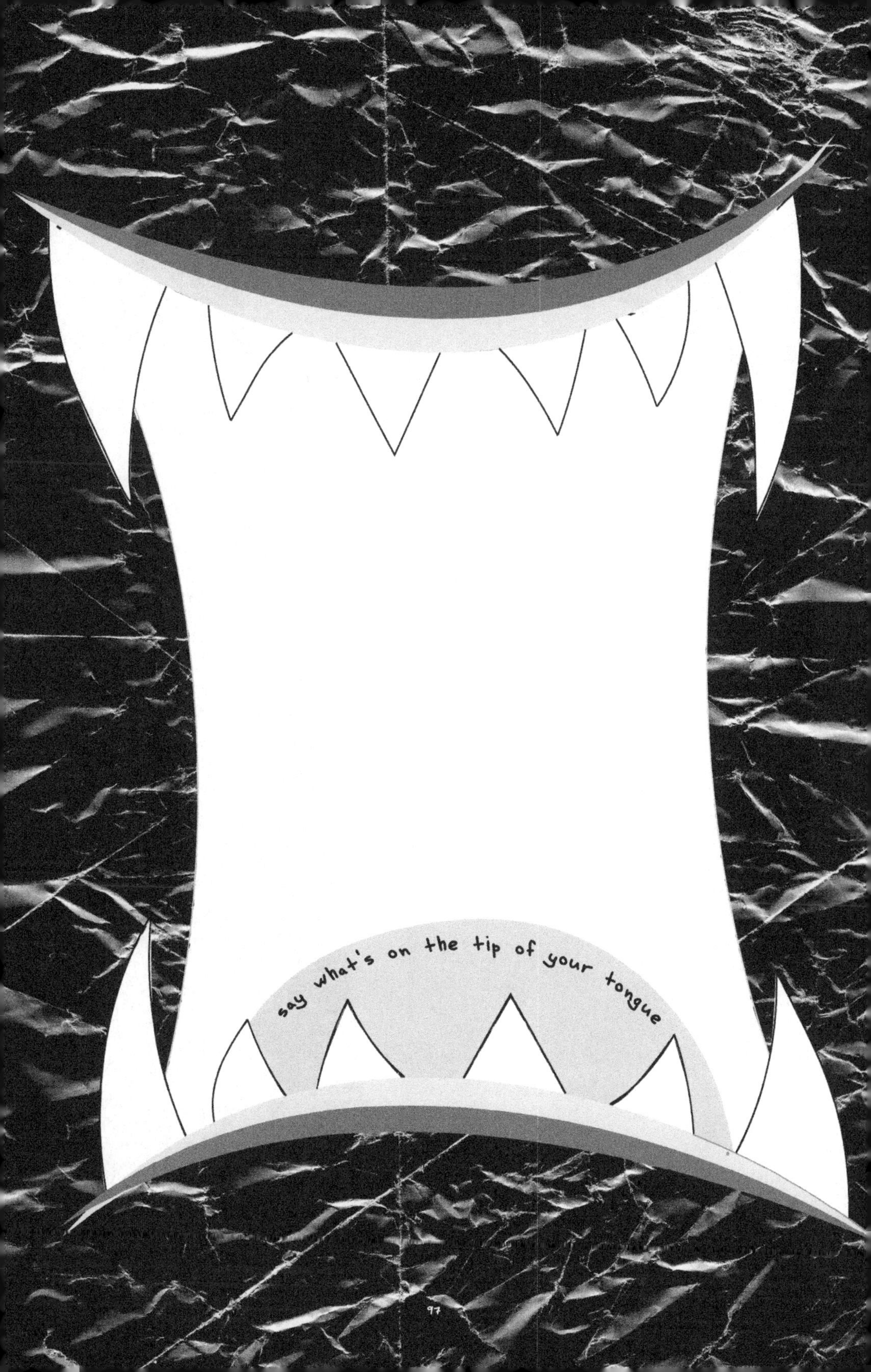

say what's on the tip of your tongue

shine a light on it

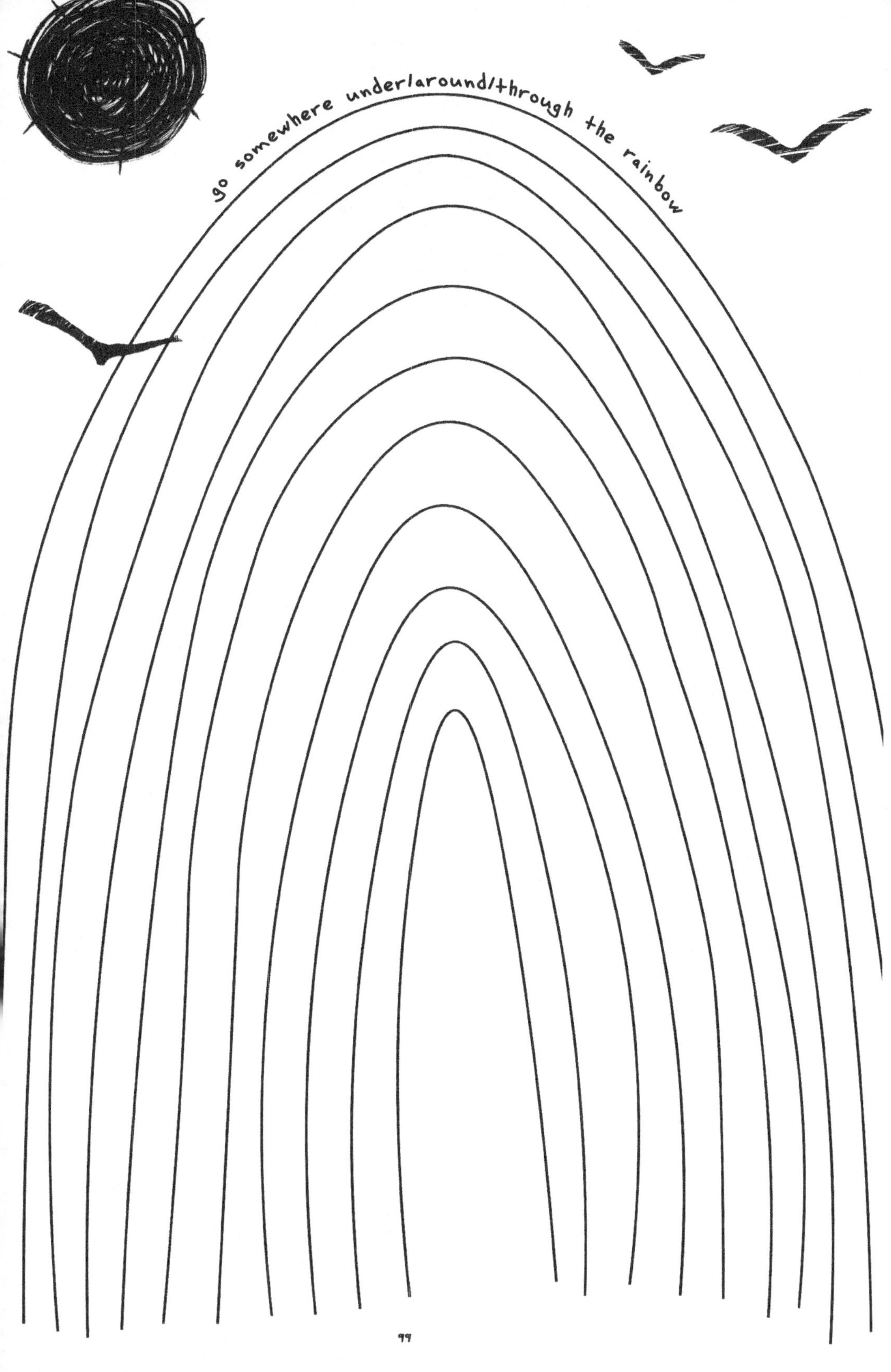

go somewhere under/around/through the rainbow

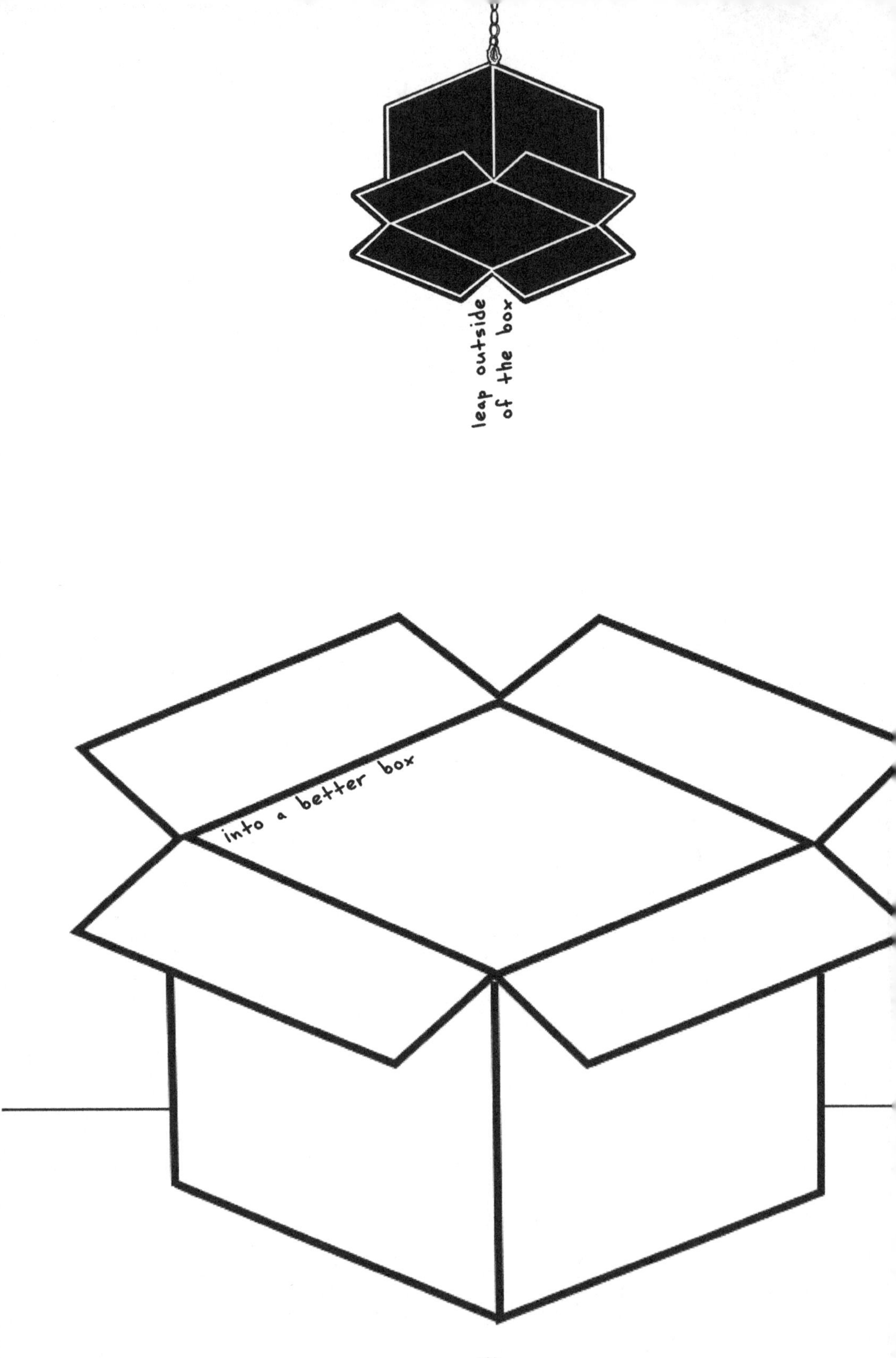

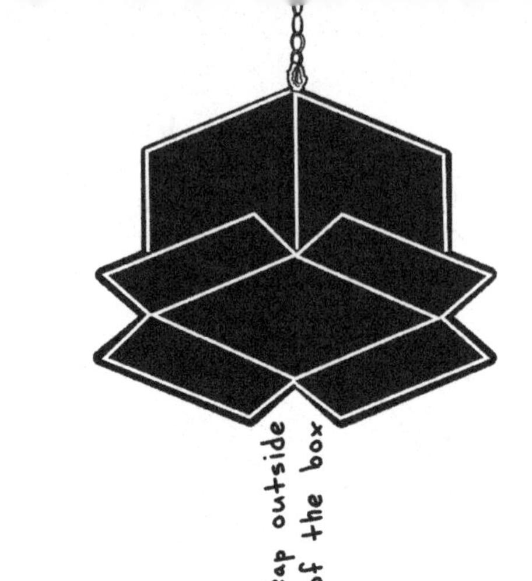
leap outside
of the box

into a better box

write yourself out of a corner

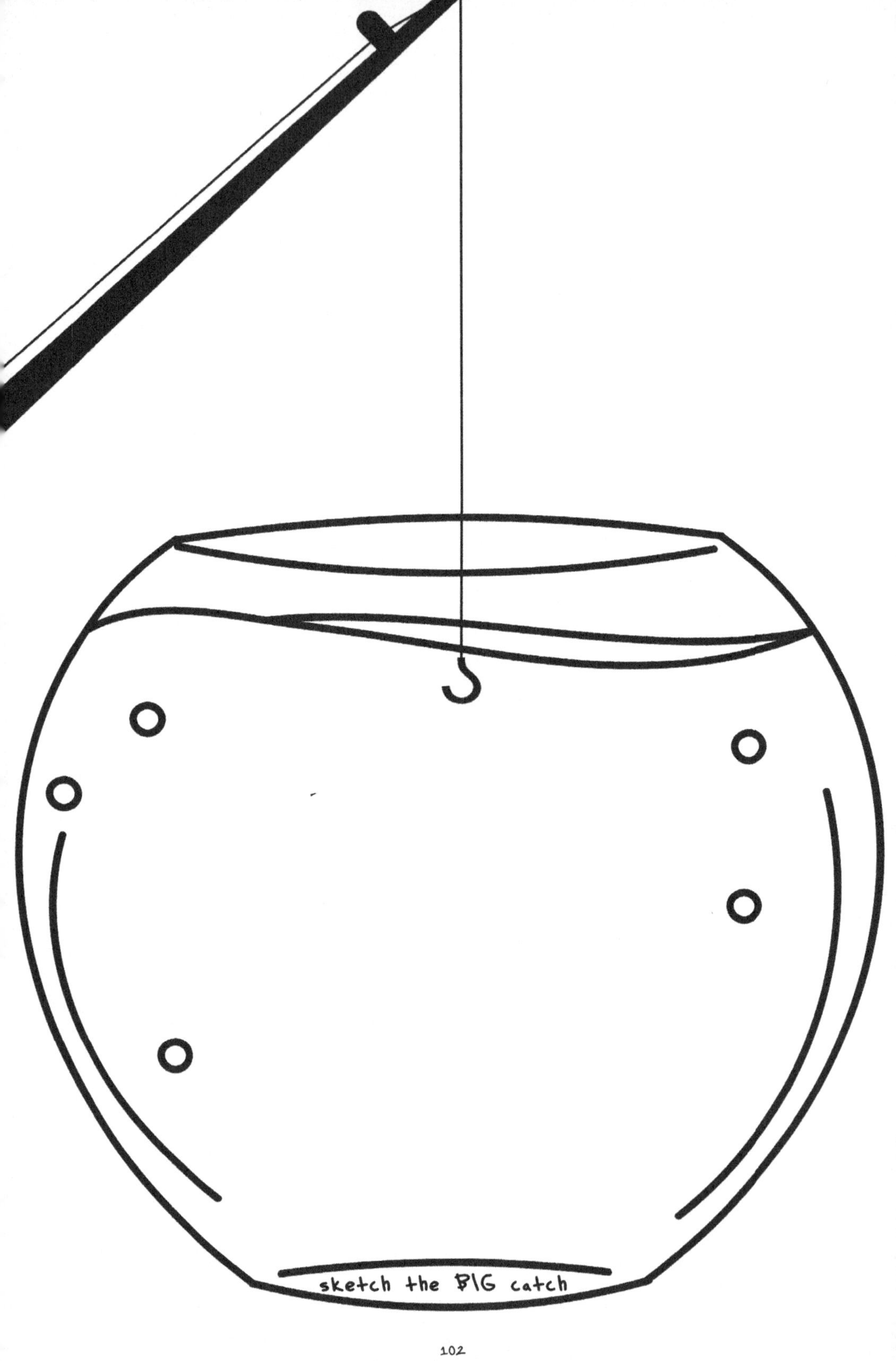

sketch the BIG catch

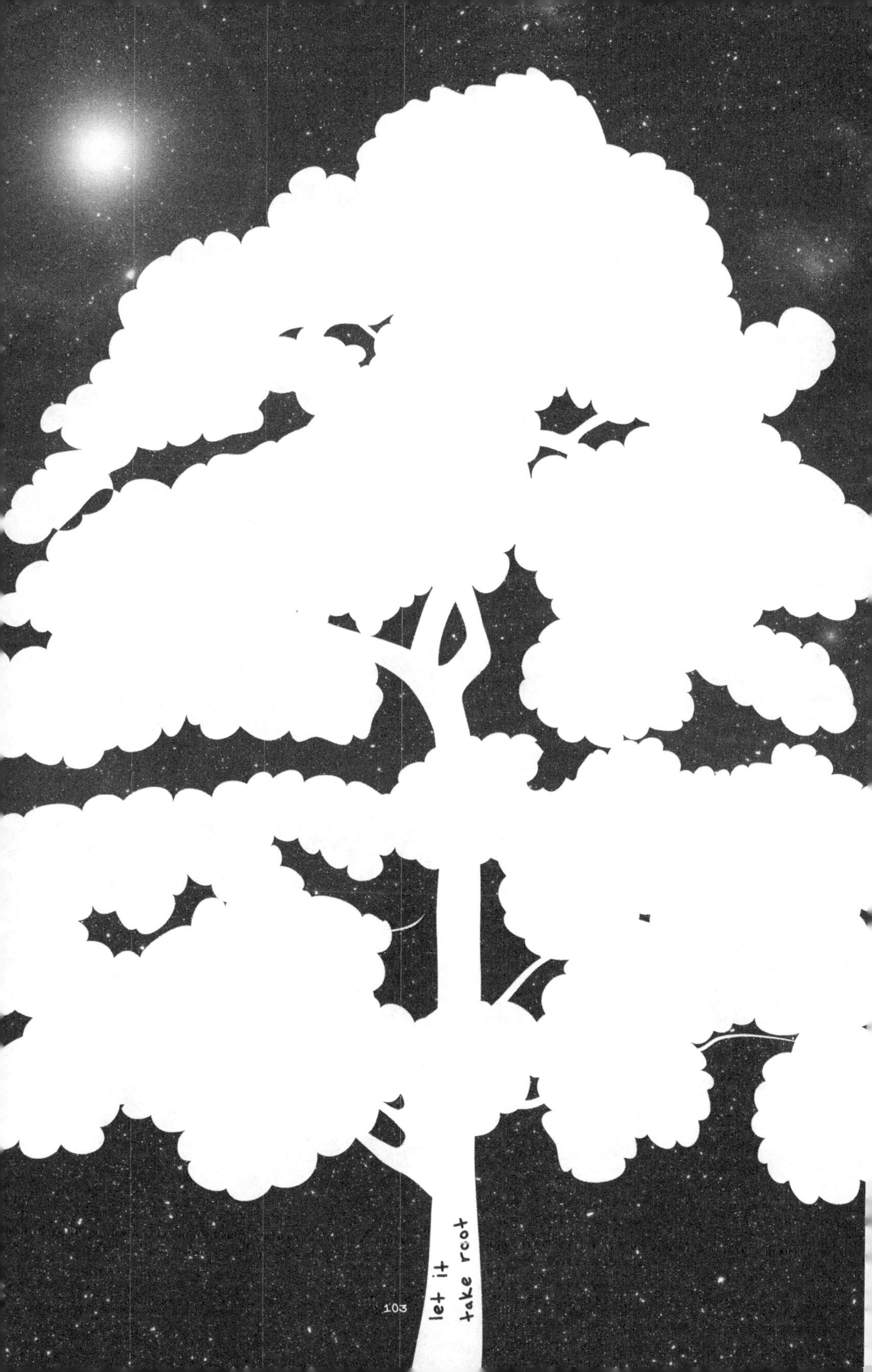
103
let it
take root

un-redact it

turn it upside down

negate the scribbles

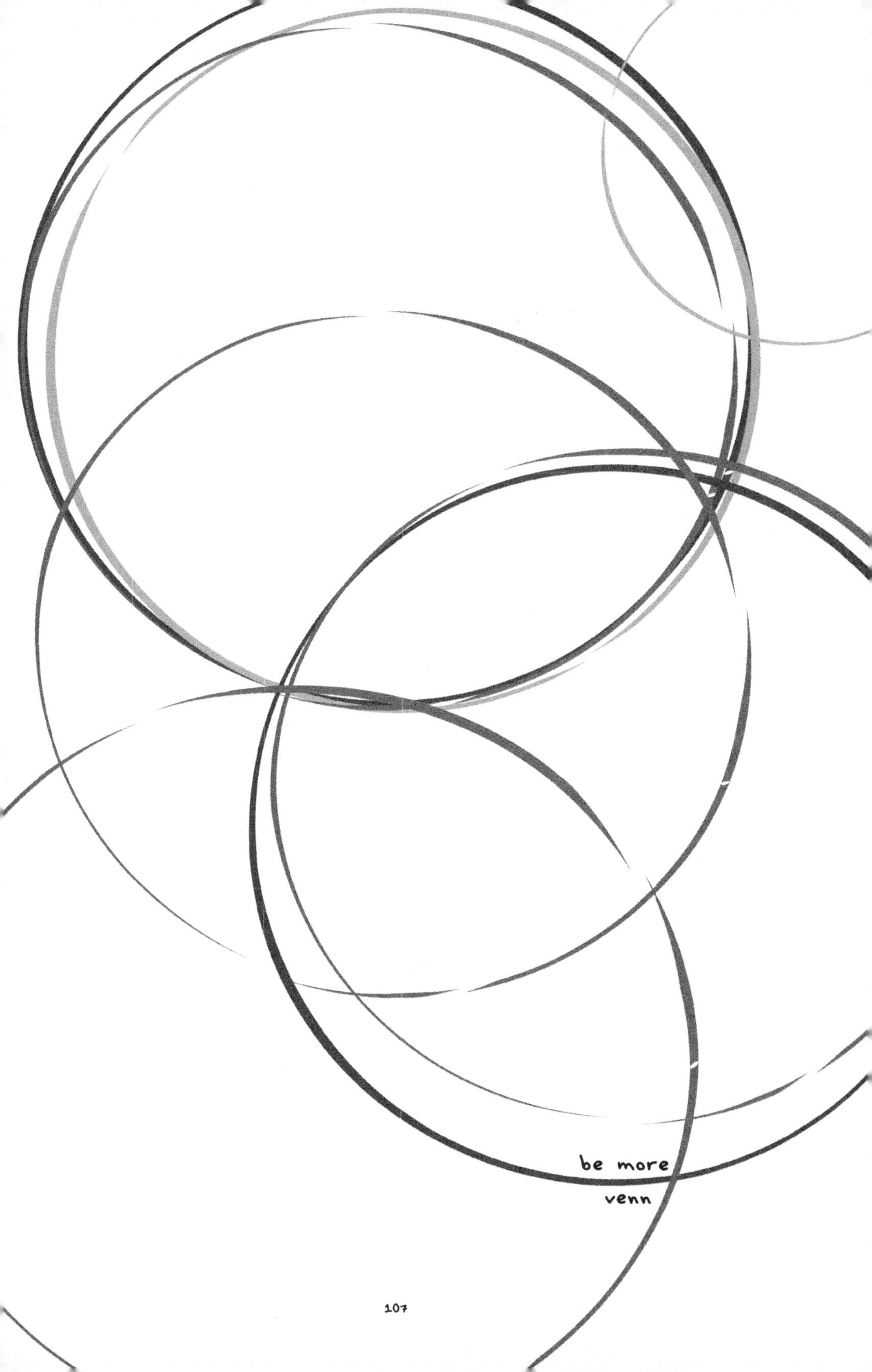
be more
venn

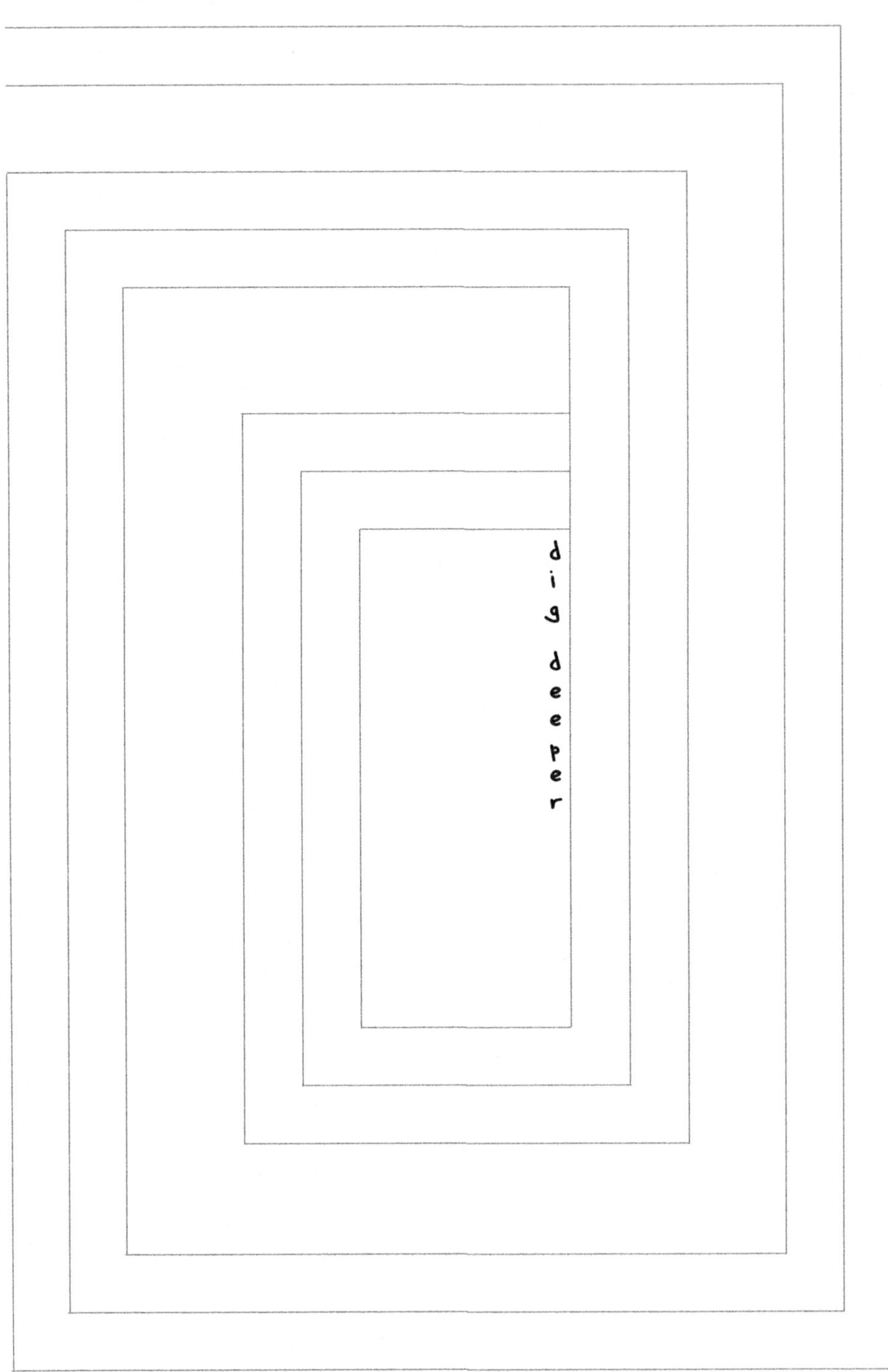

dig deeper

have a proper brainstorm

vandalize it

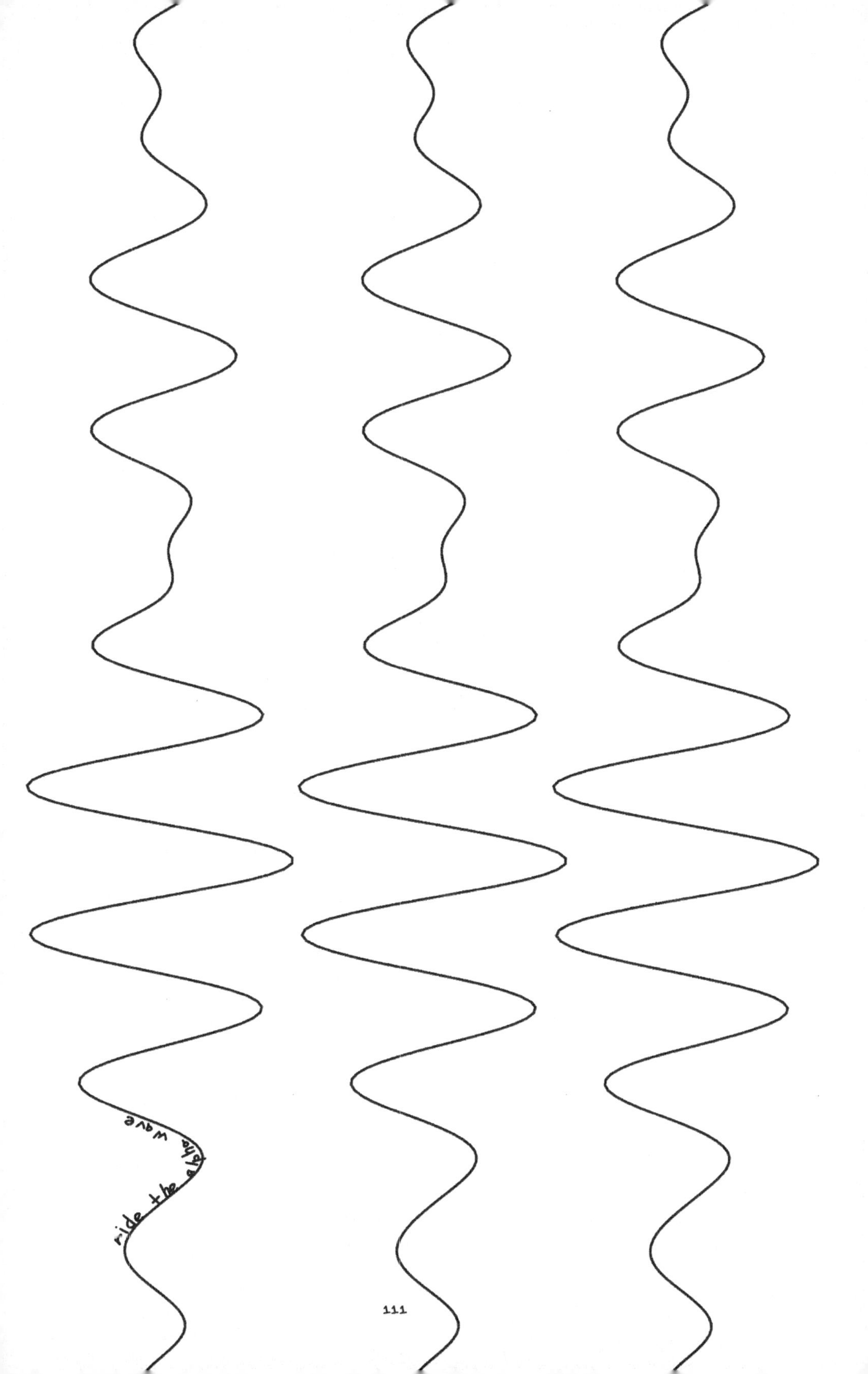

ride the wave

set
it on
fire

SAY.BLURT.SPILLIT.TELL.BEG.SCREAM.UTTER.PROCLAIM.EXPRESS.SPEAK.SHOUT.WHISPER.SPEW.AIRIT.YELL.CRYOUT.EXPLAIN.HOLLER.ECHO.BLARE.VOCALIZE.SPITITOUT.

STATE.PLEAD.BLABBER.MOUTH.COMMENT.SPOUT.REWORD.VENT.VOICE.DISCUSS.ARTICULATE.MUMBLE.SPIN.COMMENT.BLABBER.SAY.BLURT.REWORD.SPILLIT.ARTICULATE.TELL.

ANNOUNCE.BEG.SNARL.SCREAM.ELABORATE.UTTER.PROCLAIM.VENT.EXPRESS.SPEAK.SPOUT.STATE.SHOUT.WHISPER.SPEW.PLEAD.AIR.YELL.CRYOUT.EXPLAIN.DECLARE.HOLLER.

DISCUSS.ECHO.BLARE.VOCALIZE.SPITITOUT.MOUTH.VOICE.ADMIT.SAY.BLURT.SPILLIT.TELL.BEG.SCREAM.UTTER.PROCLAIM.EXPRESS.SPEAK.SHOUT.WHISPER.SPEW.AIRIT.

YELL.CRYOUT.EXPLAIN.HOLLER.ECHO.BLARE.VOCALIZE.SPITITOUT.STATE.PLEAD.BLABBER.MOUTH.COMMENT.SPOUT.REWORD.VENT.VOICE.DISCUSS.ARTICULATE.MUMBLE.SPIN.

COMMENT.BLABBER.SAY.BLURT.REWORD.SPILLIT.ARTICULATE.TELL.ANNOUNCE.BEG.ADMIT.SNARL.SCREAM.ELABORATE.UTTER.PROCLAIM.VENT.EXPRESS.SPEAK.SPOUT.STATE.

SHOUT.WHISPER.SPEW.PLEAD.AIR.YELL.CRYOUT.EXPLAIN.DECLARE.HOLLER.DISCUSS.ECHO.BLARE.VOCALIZE.SPITITOUT.MOUTH.VOICE.SAY.BLURT.SPILLIT.TELL.BEG.SCREAM.

UTTER.PROCLAIM.EXPRESS.SPEAK.SHOUT.WHISPER.SPEW.AIRIT.YELL.CRYOUT.EXPLAIN.HOLLER.ECHO.BLARE.VOCALIZE.SPITITOUT.STATE.PLEAD.BLABBER.MOUTH.COMMENT.SPOUT.

REWORD.VENT.VOICE.DISCUSS.ARTICULATE.ADMIT.MUMBLE.SPIN.COMMENT.BLABBER.SAY.BLURT.REWORD.SPILLIT.ARTICULATE.TELL.ANNOUNCE.BEG.SNARL.SCREAM.ELABORATE.

UTTER.PROCLAIM.VENT.EXPRESS.SPEAK.SPOUT.STATE.SHOUT.WHISPER.SPEW.PLEAD.AIR.YELL.CRYOUT.EXPLAIN.DECLARE.HOLLER.DISCUSS.ECHO.BLARE.VOCALIZE.SPITITOUT.

MOUTH.VOICE.SAY.BLURT.SPILLIT.TELL.BEG.SCREAM.UTTER.PROCLAIM.EXPRESS.SPEAK.SHOUT.WHISPER.SPEW.AIRIT.YELL.CRYOUT.EXPLAIN.HOLLER.ECHO.BLARE.

VOCALIZE.SPITITOUT.STATE.PLEAD.BLABBER.MOUTH.COMMENT.SPOUT.REWORD.VENT.VOICE.DISCUSS.ARTICULATE.MUMBLE.SPIN.COMMENT.BLABBER.SAY.BLURT.REWORD.SPILLIT.

ARTICULATE.TELL.ANNOUNCE.BEG.SNARL.SCREAM.ELABORATE.UTTER.PROCLAIM.VENT.EXPRESS.SPEAK.SPOUT.STATE.SHOUT.WHISPER.SPEW.PLEAD.AIR.YELL.CRYOUT.

EXPLAIN.DECLARE.HOLLER.DISCUSS.ECHO.BLARE.VOCALIZE.SPITITOUT.MOUTH.VOICE.SAY.BLURT.SPILLIT.SUGGEST.TELL.BEG.SCREAM.UTTER.PROCLAIM.EXPRESS.SPEAK.SHOUT.

WHISPER.SPEW.AIRIT.YELL.CRYOUT.EXPLAIN.HOLLER.ECHO.BLARE.VOCALIZE.SPITITOUT.STATE.PLEAD.BLABBER.MOUTH.COMMENT.SPOUT.REWORD.VENT.VOICE.DISCUSS.

ARTICULATE.MUMBLE.SPIN.COMMENT.BLABBER.SAY.BLURT.REWORD.SPILLIT.ARTICULATE.TELL.ANNOUNCE.BEG.SNARL.SCREAM.ELABORATE.UTTER.PROCLAIM.VENT.EXPRESS.SPEAK.

SPOUT.STATE.SHOUT.WHISPER.SPEW.PLEAD.AIR.YELL.CRYOUT.EXPLAIN.DECLARE.HOLLER.DISCUSS.ECHO.BLARE.VOCALIZE.SPITITOUT.MOUTH.VOICE.SAY.BLURT.SPILLIT.

TELL.BEG.SCREAM.UTTER.PROCLAIM.EXPRESS.SUGGEST.SPEAK.SHOUT.WHISPER.SPEW.AIRIT.YELL.CRYOUT.EXPLAIN.HOLLER.ECHO.BLARE.VOCALIZE.SPITITOUT.STATE.PLEAD.

BLABBER.ADMIT.MOUTH.COMMENT.SPOUT.REWORD.VENT.VOICE.DISCUSS.ARTICULATE.MUMBLE.SPIN.COMMENT.BLABBER.SAY.BLURT.REWORD.SPILLIT.ARTICULATE.TELL.

ANNOUNCE.BEG.SNARL.SCREAM.ELABORATE.UTTER.PROCLAIM.VENT.EXPRESS.SPEAK.SPOUT.STATE.SHOUT.WHISPER.SPEW.PLEAD.AIR.YELL.CRYOUT.EXPLAIN.SUGGEST.DECLARE.

HOLLER.DISCUSS.ECHO.BLARE.VOCALIZE.SPITITOUT.MOUTH.VOICE.SAY.BLURT.SPILLIT.TELL.BEG.SCREAM.UTTER.PROCLAIM.EXPRESS.SPEAK.SHOUT.WHISPER.SPEW.AIRIT.YELL.

CRYOUT.EXPLAIN.HOLLER.ECHO.ADMIT.BLARE.VOCALIZE.SPITITOUT.STATE.PLEAD.BLABBER.MOUTH.COMMENT.SPOUT.REWORD.VENT.VOICE.DISCUSS.ARTICULATE.MUMBLE.SPIN.

COMMENT.BLABBER.SAY.BLURT.REWORD.SPILLIT.ARTICULATE.TELL.ANNOUNCE.BEG.SNARL.SCREAM.ELABORATE.UTTER.PROCLAIM.VENT.EXPRESS.SPEAK.SPOUT.STATE.SHOUT.

WHISPER.ADMIT.SPEW.PLEAD.AIR.YELL.CRYOUT.EXPLAIN.DECLARE.HOLLER.DISCUSS.ECHO.BLARE.VOCALIZE.SPITITOUT.MOUTH.VOICE.SAY.BLURT.SPILLIT.TELL.BEG.SCREAM.

UTTER.PROCLAIM.EXPRESS.SPEAK.SHOUT.WHISPER.SPEW.AIRIT.YELL.CRYOUT.EXPLAIN.HOLLER.ECHO.BLARE.VOCALIZE.SPITITOUT.STATE.PLEAD.BLABBER.MOUTH.COMMENT.

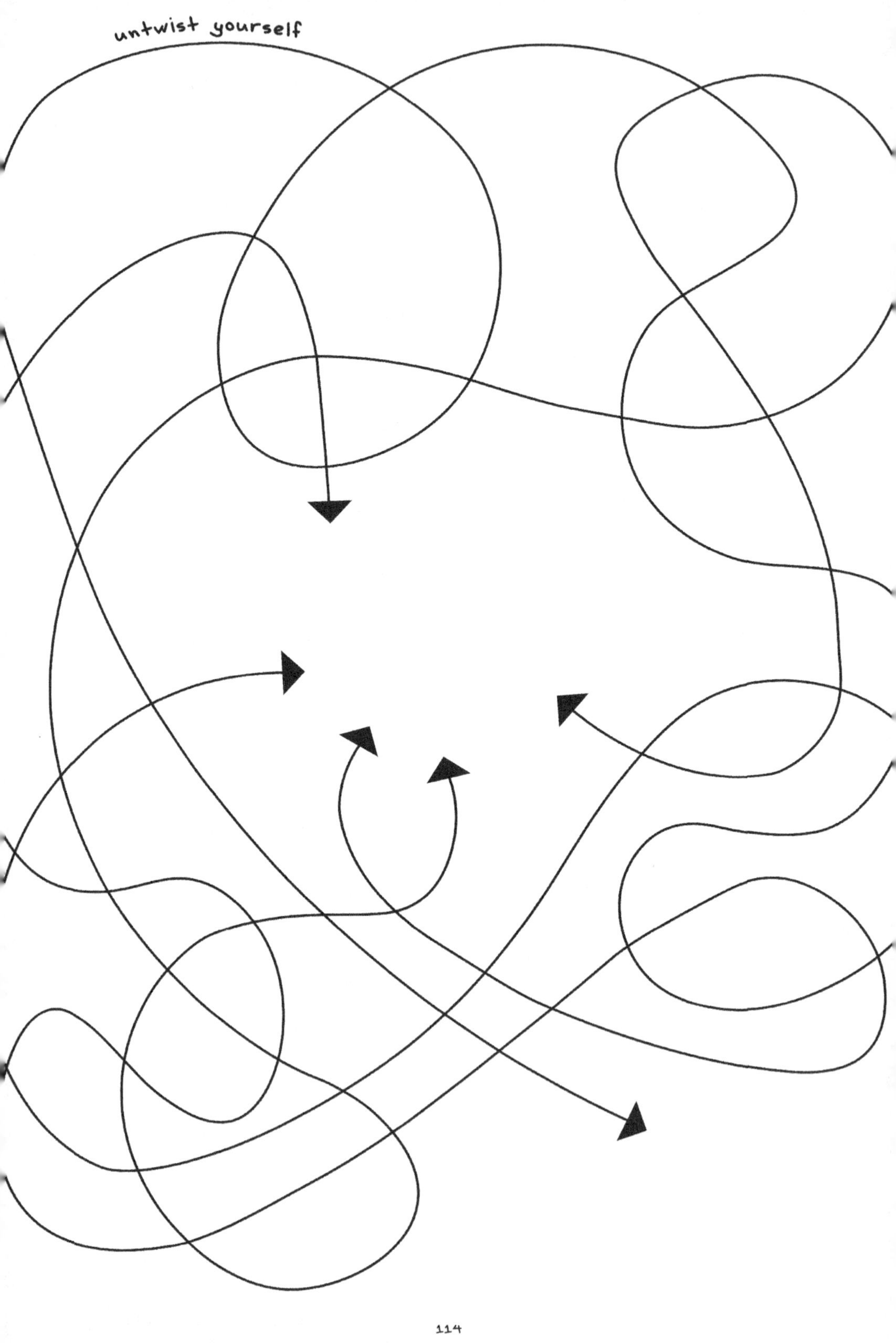
untwist yourself

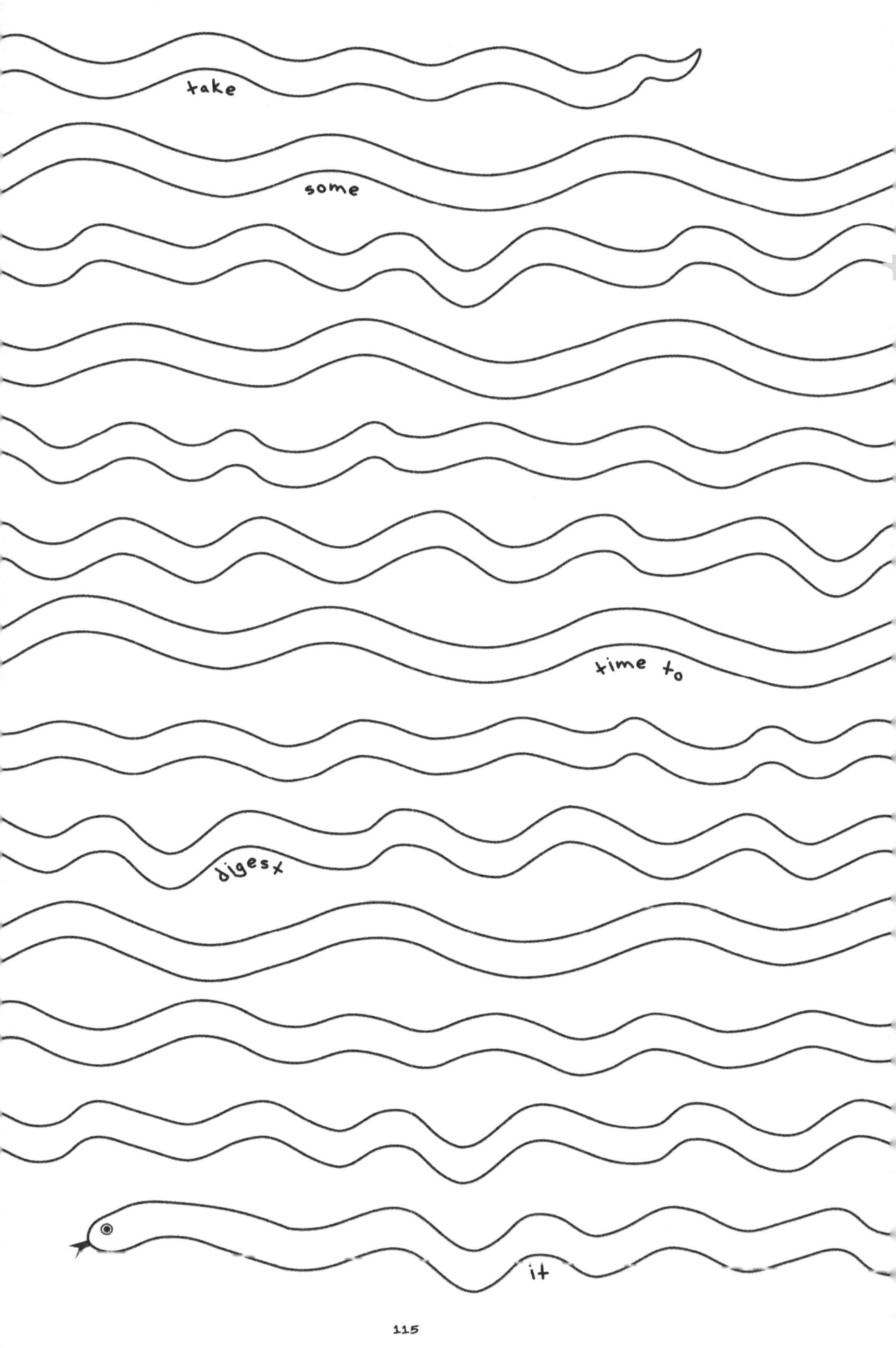

take
some
time to
digest
some
it

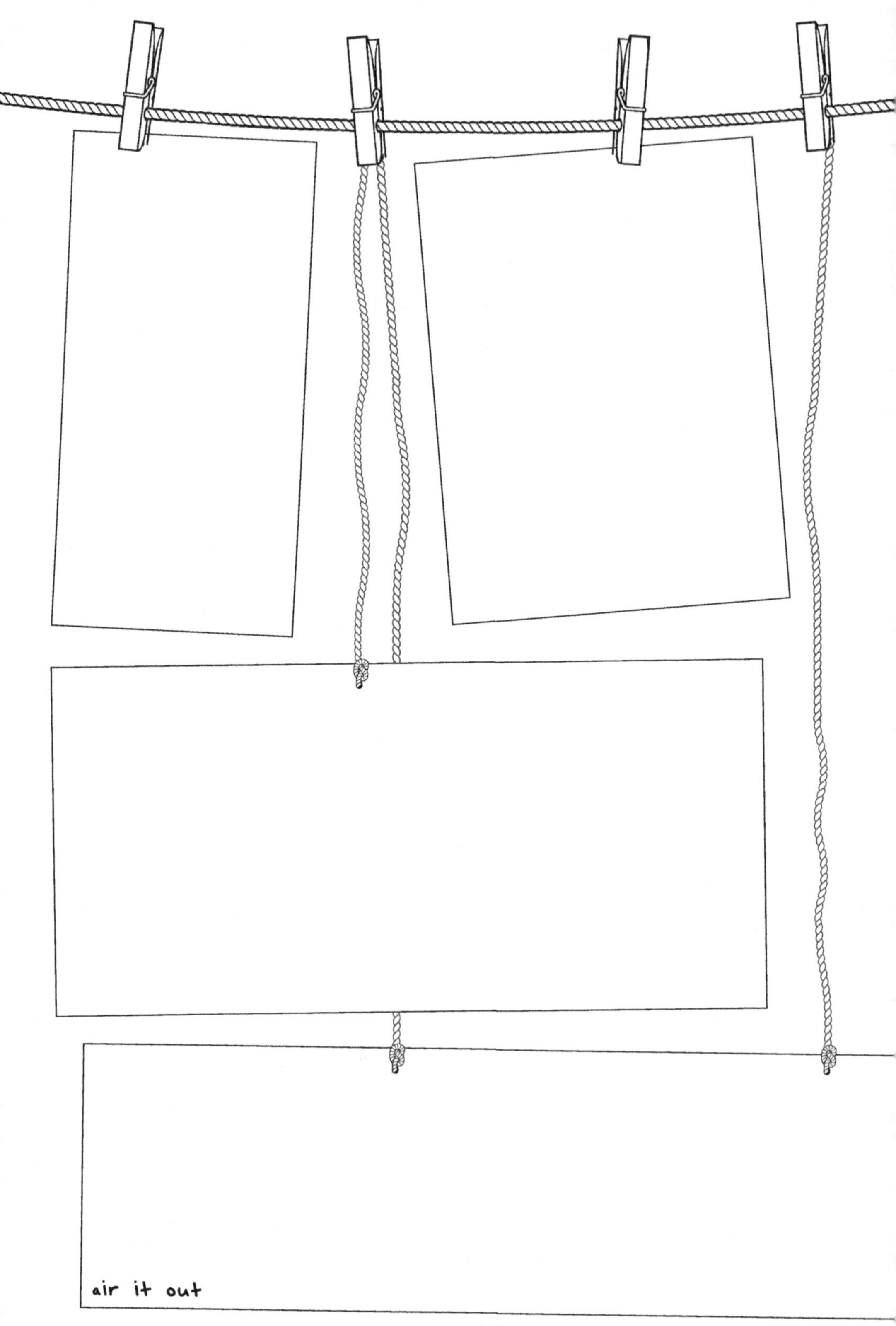

air it out
air it out

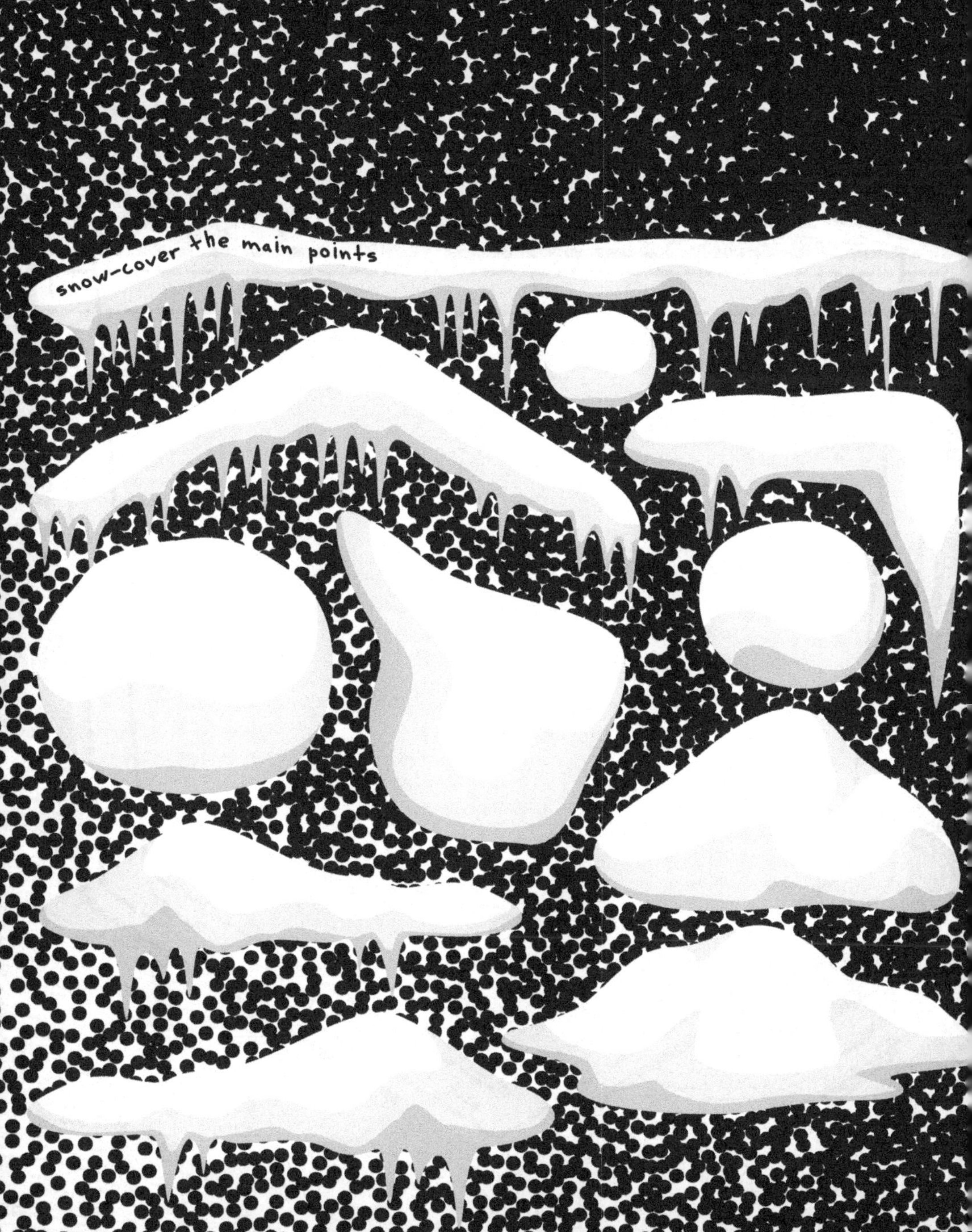

snow-cover the main points
the main points

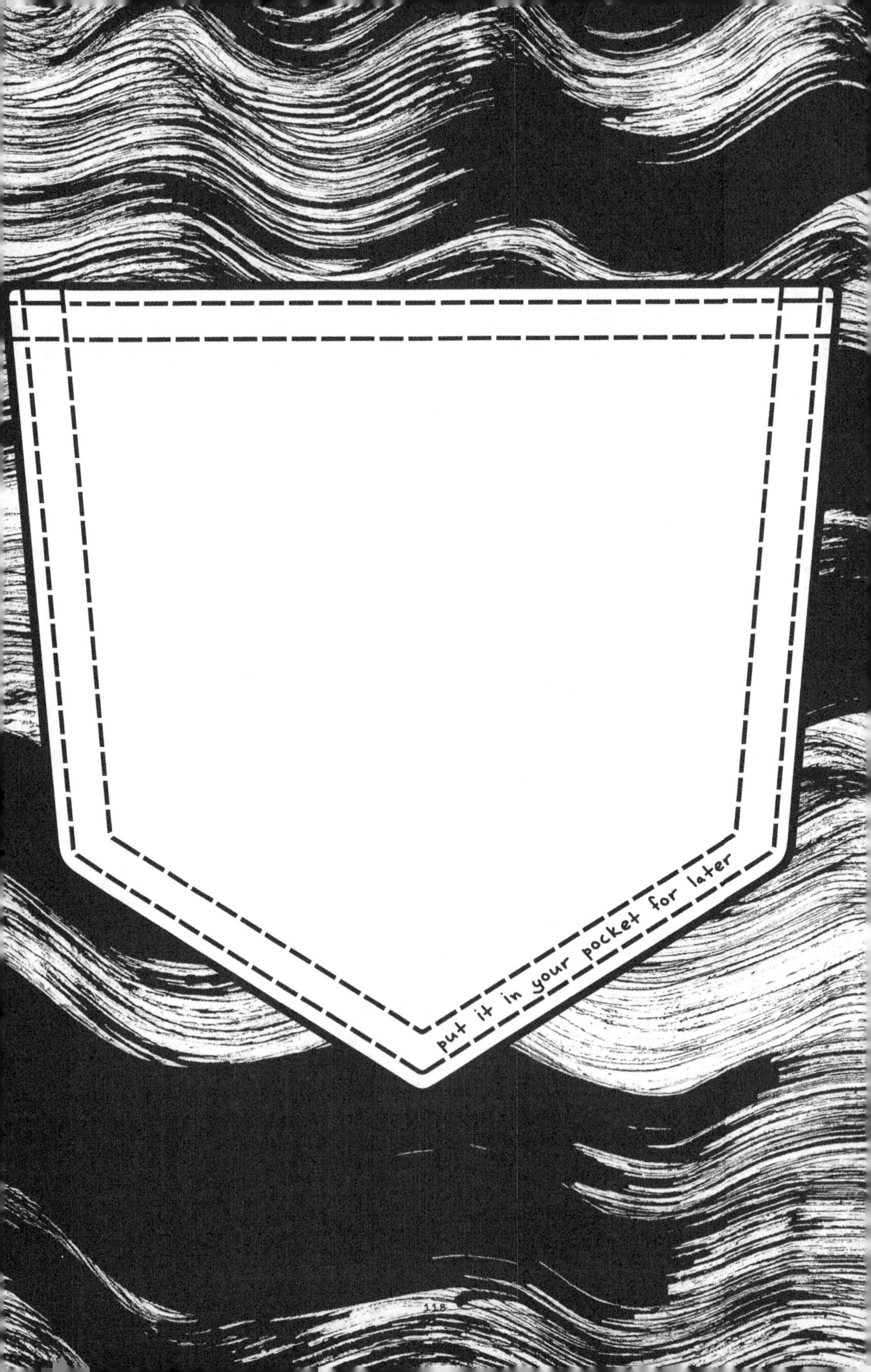

put it in your pocket for later

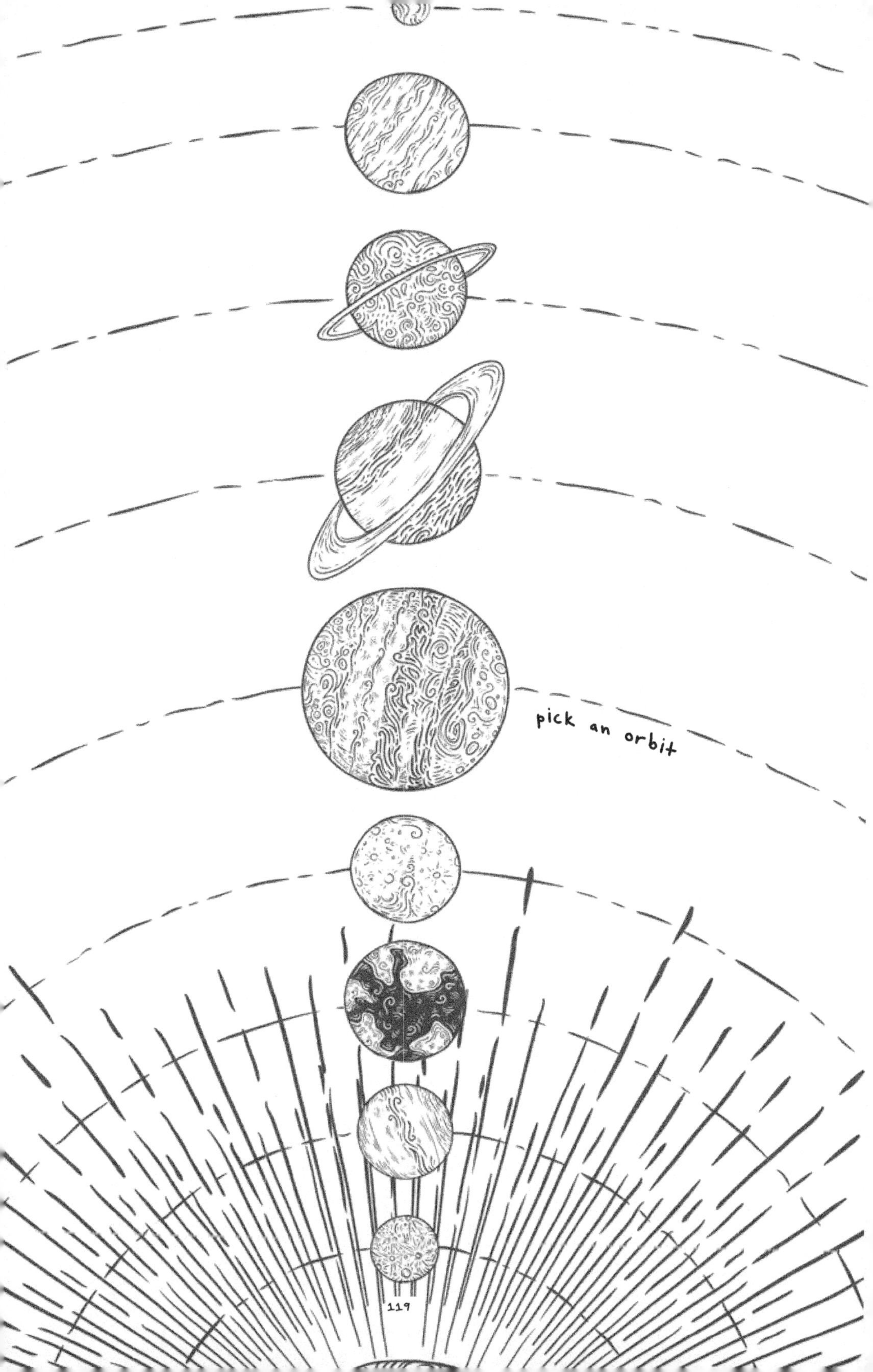
pick an orbit

float an idea

Made in the USA
Las Vegas, NV
03 August 2023